# *Include Me Out!*

## CONFESSIONS OF
## AN ECCLESIASTICAL COWARD

# COLIN MORRIS

London
EPWORTH PRESS

© COLIN MORRIS 1968
FIRST PUBLISHED IN 1968
BY EPWORTH PRESS
Book Steward: Frank H. Cumbers
PRINTED IN GREAT BRITAIN
BY PAGE & THOMAS LTD
CHESHAM, BUCKINGHAMSHIRE
SECOND IMPRESSION 1968
THIRD IMPRESSION 1968
FOURTH IMPRESSION 1968
FIFTH IMPRESSION 1968
SIXTH IMPRESSION 1968
SEVENTH IMPRESSION 1968
EIGHTH IMPRESSION 1968
SBN 7612 0010 4

*Include Me Out!*

For
BILL GOWLAND
and
MERFYN TEMPLE
who *do* the job

# One

THE other day a Zambian dropped dead not a hundred yards from my front door. The pathologist said he'd died of hunger. In his shrunken stomach were a few leaves and what appeared to be a ball of grass. And nothing else.

That same day saw the arrival of my *Methodist Recorder*, an issue whose columns were electric with indignation, consternation, fever and fret at the post-ponement of the final Report of the Anglican–Methodist Unity Commission. Until that morning I had been enjoying the war that the issue had sparked off, and, indeed, had sent aloft the odd missile of my own.

It took an ugly little man with a shrunken belly, whose total possessions, according to the Police, were a pair of shorts, a ragged shirt and an empty Biro pen, to show me that this whole Union affair is the great Non-Event of recent British Church history.

For the first time I was able to see out of another's eyes. And through that pair of dead eyes all our re-organization of ecclesiastical structures had the aspect of a man spending ten years of his life building a model of Blackpool Tower from a million matchsticks. Any sane person's reaction to such a feat is made up of equal parts admiration for dogged tenacity and amazement at the utter uselessness of the project. But tell the man that the whole thing seems somewhat of a waste of time and energy and you would be asking for trouble.

That magnificent grotesque structure has value for him. He has gone on, through hail and sun and snow and sleet, sticking those little bits of wood together. It is both a genuine labour of love and a classical example of Marxist economics – its sole value lies in the labour that has been invested in it. But it is not worth a fiver at the nearest pawn shop, because the world doesn't happen to be perishing for lack of match-stick models of the Blackpool Tower.

Nor is the world perishing for lack of stronger, better organized Churches. It is perishing for lack of bread. That little man was a well-publicized statistic. He was one of those two out of three members of the human race who are not asking with bated breath 'Is that Service really re-ordination?' or 'How will the Methodist Conference vote?' They ask a simpler question 'Where does my next meal come from?' The bread they are interested in is not that, covered by a fair linen cloth, over which the theologians argue, but the other sort that eases a gnawing pain in the belly.

I hear that at one debate on the Anglican–Methodist Union Scheme there was a long and anxious discussion about the disposal of the bread after Communion. When a layman suggested feeding the birds with it, some Bishop recoiled in horror, pointing out to the theological cretin that since the bread had been set apart for ever, it must be disposed of in a very special

8

way – the priest had to eat it. There must be a parable in that picture of a priest gorging himself on the Bread of Life in a hungry world.

Who Kiddeth Whom? It's all like one of those nightmare games played with utter intensity by the inmates of a lunatic asylum, their laughter and anger cut off from people walking down the street by the padded walls of their cells. And just as lunatics have been known to do violence over the turn of a card or the throw of dice, so that Church has its long and glorious roll of idiot-heroes who have gone happily to the stake for their convictions over such questions as whether or not bread remains bread after it has been consecrated at altar or communion table.

Because precious blood has been spilt over such issues, they assume terrible importance to us who, more often than not by sheer accident of birth, follow the path trodden by these martyrs. All the Church's martyrdoms have not been such exercises in utter futility, but too many have. And private feuds do not achieve moral significance merely because men are prepared to spill blood, their own or their opponents', over them. You *can* die in defence of Paul's assertion that women should wear hats in Church but all the blood and fire and anguish will not redeem the issue from triviality, any more than a solid gold frame will transform a chimpanzee's scribblings into an Old Master.

To put one's life on the line for a handful of dust, and in loyalty to a long procession of others who have given their lives for the same dust, is not martyrdom. It is lunacy in the strict sense of the word – the refusal or inability to see the world as it really is. So we go on our merry way, spending our anger and righteousness

9

and conviction in pursuit of strictly private obsessions, observed by a world whose astonishment gradually subsides into boredom. There is only limited entertainment value in watching someone swallowing razor blades, even when he announces between each mouthful that everyone would be the healthier for following the same diet.

Thus the Interim Report: 'Various important issues relating to Holy Communion, including those concerned with Open Communion as practised in the Methodist Church, the use of fermented wine and the reverent disposal of consecrated elements, are under active consideration, and our judgement on these matters will find a place in the Final Report.' So thousands of intelligent, fully grown men and women will hang in an agony of indecision about the Union until they hear the glad word that the communion wine will be non-alcoholic and birds will not get the bread. Leaving aside the obvious fact that neither issue would have been of the slightest interest to Jesus, for whose sake all this ferment and fret is being endured, there is as much plain horse-sense in such suspension of decision as in someone refusing to come in out of the rain until we reassure him about the colour of our bathroom tiles.

Certainly our fathers thought such matters were worth suffering and dying for. They also fought over whether the Earth was round or flat, at what point a girl-foetus developed a soul, and whether hangmen could be saved. And they put seamen into the stocks for kissing their wives goodbye in public on the Sabbath Day. It may be hindsight to claim more wisdom than they had, but we are only permitted to squeeze back into the Ptolemaic Universe or re-stage the Battle of Bannockburn if we adopt the right of infants, the retired and the insane to pursue private interests without public accountability. And patient though God may be with our nursery antics, He is unlikely to allow that degree of detachment in His people.

And so I have undergone something of a conversion on the question of Anglican–Methodist Union. Not from Pro. to Con. or vice versa. But to a sort of functional neutrality in that I don't give a damn which way the vote goes so long as we get the whole business out of the way and regain our sanity. Either side can buy my vote for a quid's donation to Oxfam. Unity, like every other aspect of the business of organized Christianity, is a tool and we have turned it into an obsession. One is reminded of that Baluba village in the Congo, whose inhabitants were so impressed by their first sight of the common or garden shovel that they added it to the pantheon of their gods.

I am, of course, aware of the argument that runs: this Union may not, in itself, directly affect the plight of those hungry two out of three. But it will give us a stronger base from which to fulfil our mission, one aspect of which is the alleviation of the world's suffering. I know that argument well, because I have used it *ad nauseam*. Not any more, because it simply is not true. In itself, one big Church has no more value than two small ones, just as a shilling has no more value than two sixpences.

I beg leave to doubt those optimistic claims that once we have got Anglican–Methodist Union out of the way we can roll up our sleeves and get down to the real job, for by that time we shall virtually have forgotten what the real job is. Wasn't it Bob Hope who said 'Familiarity breeds . . .'? That's it in a nutshell. This sort of thing, like the simplest form of life, is self-propagating. One generation of ministers having gone to their rest after spending themselves in clearing the way for Union, another generation will leave theological colleges destined to occupy a forty year stint, health permitting, clearing their way through the accumulated bric-a-brac of property, finance, redundancy and administrative problems that Union will bring in its wake.

Like every other hobby, ecclesiastical joinery offers the lure of progressing from the elementary to the elaborate. Having cut our teeth on the Anglicans, there will be the Roman Catholics to take on. And because they are bigger and the issues are graver, that's a contest that should go the full distance and see the Century out. So the fun starts all over again.

Not for me it doesn't. It takes much of the point out of playing Cowboys and Indians if one kid lies down and insists on being dead before anyone shoots at him. That's me. I am the classical ecclesiastical coward. There is barely a single one of those great questions at present convulsing the Church that is worth fighting over. So I shall capitulate without a struggle.

I don't really care whether I end up in a Union Church or as a residual Methodist. I don't really care whether I am ordained, re-ordained, reconciled or commissioned by Bishops, Presidents, priests or presbyters. I don't care *where* they put the Words of Absolution, so long as there is some point in the Service at which I can unload my conscience, over-burdened with the knowledge of what we have done to that little man with the shrunken belly in the name of Christ.

I don't even care in what sense Holy Communion is to be regarded as a Sacrifice, for it's all a play on words

– the special use of a private vocabulary to lend meaning to a ritual, parts of which long ago lost any contact with reality. For real sacrifices, like all genuine crucifixions, take place, not on the altar but outside the Jerusalems of this world.

And I'm willing to go through that Service of Reconciliation kneeling, standing, sitting or lying flat on my face if it will make some dear souls happy. If that rigmarole can add anything by way of authority to what God has already given me, I shall be humbly grateful; for as sure as fate it can't take anything away.

Is it not time we distinguished between what is genuine and what is spurious in our present concerns? Much of our anxiety as ministers to safeguard the validity of our Orders stems from nothing other than personal vanity – the 'I'm-every-bit-as-good-as-you' syndrome. And much lay protestation about loyalty to the tradition of their fathers is sheer vested interest. It has no more theological significance than the local grocer's desire to go on bossing up his own little show rather than managing a branch of a bigger one – a perfectly reasonable thing to want to do, provided he does not claim that God, too, is partial to the one-man business.

'We are those who must be content with the lowest places at the Feast', we thunder from our pulpits, and go on to point out that Jesus' view of greatness demands a willingness to become of no account. Then we hurry off to the next Unity meeting, grimly determined as a matter of honour to secure for our side a reasonable share of seats at the top table. True, the Other Side do it too! But they must make their own peace with those terrible words of Jesus. Our theological claims may be beyond question, but our attitudes are often more in line with a Company take-over struggle than an operation to heal the wounds of the Body of Christ – except that not even the most hard-bitten industrial tycoon would claim to be casting God's shares by proxy.

When we have finished laying down conditions and demanding this, that, or the other thing, as the price of Union, we have the right to make only a single claim, and it has nothing directly to do with episcopal government or the nature of the priesthood. We can demand of any ecclesiastical structure that it give us the freedom to minister. And unless words have lost their meaning, a minister is simply one who is humanely useful. Many of the subtleties we claim to be able to detect in that term are far remote from Jesus' down-to-earth use of it. They are theological barnacles accumulated over a very long time and in the usual way – through loitering too long in stagnant waters.

If I am not humanely useful to the life of the world then the laying on of hands of every Bishop in Christendom will not validate my ministry. And if I manage some degree of usefulness then the theological significance of what I do is vested solely in my action and not in my status.

I know of no compelling arguments against Church Union, just as I know of no compelling arguments against clearing up the litter in the park or straightening the papers on my desk or giving the Westminster Central Hall a face-lift. Nor do I think the issue is worth more than a comparable expenditure of energy. A hard week-end's bargaining to decide what to do with our assets would be a little hurried, I grant, but a month's talking is extravagance, a year's arguing is dereliction of duty and five years of it is sheer infantilism – the Freudian desire to creep back into the womb of Great Mother Church, having first demanded that we be given our identical pre-natal position.

To put the issue so starkly is to be accused of the offence, heinous in any Christian and unforgivable in a parson, of not taking theology seriously. So be it. It doesn't seem to me that the bulk of what passes for theology, including the odd book I have inflicted on the public, has the slightest use or value except to those who make their living writing and teaching it. How little we have to show for the vast mountain of theological works that litter our shelves, spill over on to the floor and into the attic. The wild joy of the prospector who lights upon a diamond after sifting acres of sludge is no greater than the delight of the average Christian when in a mountain of verbiage he spots a sentence he can understand, let alone do something about.

Much theological writing is a highly elaborate conspiracy against that little man with the shrunken belly and his skeletal brethren. It is an exercise in endless qualification, dedicated to showing why we cannot take the words of the Galilean Peasant at their face value or follow His example simply.

Let some Manchester bus conductor murmur that he can follow the words of Jesus but cannot follow the words of the men who followed Him and he will earn himself a lecture. This would be to the effect that Jesus cannot be understood except within the whole framework of the History of Salvation and that He did not actually say many of the words reported of Him in the Gospels, so he must take our words for what is fact and what fancy, because we *know*!

It is hazardous to take seriously the simplest saying of

15

Our Lord until the best authorities have explained its second and third meanings. Just as Medicine has almost reached the stage of specialization where different surgeons are needed to remove left and right tonsils, so any simple Christian affirmation is suspect until the Aramaists, Old and New Testament experts, the Systematic Theologians and Church historians have looked it over. And now, God help us, we have to feed Jesus' words into the Glasgow University computer to be on the safe side.

That story about the two psychiatrists who meet, and one says 'Good morning!' and the other thinks 'I wonder what he meant by that?' could be an imaginative description of an encounter between Jesus and an eminent theologian.

I pick up the nearest book to hand, which, believe it or not, is a volume of Karl Barth's *Church Dogmatics*. (And here, be it said, I am not being deliberately selective in order to suit the purposes of my argument. Barth seems to me to have the gift, rare amongst theologians of his eminence, of writing with great beauty and simplicity.) It would be quite unfair to quote one of the more complicated passages, for it is, after all, a technical work for specialists. The first fairly simple sentence my eye lights upon reads: 'Jesus is immanent in the Church only because He transcends it.'

In everyday speech this is like saying that something is wet only because it is dry, near only because it is far away and relevant only because it is irrelevant . . .

. . . Ah, breathes the theologian, that is paradox and, therefore, profound.

. . . Ah, says the man in the pew, it's beyond me but I'll take the parson's word that it means something.

. . . So what? says the man in the street, it has nothing to do with the price of fish! – a remark calculated to touch a theologian on the raw; say that he's unintelligible and he will take it as a compliment, but suggest that he is also irrelevant and he will sue you!

The theological word game operates like one of those weekly essay competitions in the *New Statesman*: 'Take Karl Barth's statement about the immanence and transcendence of Jesus and prove, in not more than 500 words, that it has everything to do with the price of fish.' The theologian might find the 500 word limit a handicap but he can prove the point with a verbal slickness that would earn him five years' penal servitude if employed on the wrong side of the law.

Here is the nub of the charge of a theological conspiracy against the little man with the shrunken belly. It consists in taking unintelligible sentences and paradoxical statements whose subject is Jesus and whose object is the world, and proving that they answer his anguished cry for bread. At least, they prove the case to our satisfaction. Not to his. He can't eat our words. He dies of hunger.

I have the greatest possible respect for Karl Barth's massive erudition and simple piety, but something has gone badly adrift with God's intention if it takes a projected ten massive volumes to interpret the life and words of One about whom we know so little that the hard facts could be rendered in a slim Penguin paperback.

'This is a travesty!' cries the theologian. 'Theology is as much entitled to its technical language as nuclear physics and the fact that the man in the street can follow neither does not affect their truth or value.'

17

This, in fairness, one would have to allow, if it were not for a single insight that is beyond dispute. Christianity came into being out of God's concern to bring His truth within range of the common man. The Incarnation was an operation in cosmic simplification or it was nothing. Yet what God rendered simply intelligible in Jesus Christ we have spent years obscuring behind layers of elaborately uniforming jargon. We have not only repaired the Veil of the Temple that was torn down the middle when Jesus died but have added a fireproof screen for good measure.

The philosopher or scientist is entitled to the complexities of his argument but any theological work which makes the truth of Jesus more difficult to understand instead of making it plain is not Christian, whatever else it is.

The trouble with all word games, not excluding the theological variety, is that they require intellect divorced from passion. Truly great theology unites intellect and passion in a way that has ordinary Christians marching to the stake, singing, for things that really matter. Much of the great sprawling mass of contemporary theology is dead not because the subject is rarefied but because there is no indication that the writers *feel* deeply. They have succumbed to the malaise of academic detachment. What was once their love seems to have become their business.

So obscure is much current theology that it amounts to a demand that the world should deliver its mind and conscience into our hands to an extent unprecedented since the days of the wizard, the alchemist and the witch doctor. Then we register dismay when the world tires of our word games and quits the field saying 'To hell with you!', which may or may not be a serious matter, but often adds 'and to hell with your Jesus', which most assuredly is.

Our smug unintelligibility is only matched by our impertinence. To stand up in the modern world and claim that the position taken up by the priest in saying Mass, or the method of disposing of the elements after Communion, or the way water is poured over a child's head at Baptism has anything remotely to do with the plight of those little people of the earth whom Jesus used as test cases of our sincerity, is breathtaking. If we say we make no such claim but that these things are important for the nourishment of *our* souls, then our endless quarrelling over them is as tasteless as a wrangle over a five-course dinner menu in a famine area. In the language of the economist, our input and output are so grossly out of balance that we appear like the tippling publican who is rarely open for business because he drinks away most of his stocks.

We *can* explain why a vast theological super-structure is necessary to enable us to do those acts of simple compassion that the Gospel says are our necessary response to what Jesus has done for us. But then, we can explain away anything we do, except possibly, why it is that our mountain of words brings forth only a gnat of humane action.

It may be a matter for argument whether there is such a thing as the *Simple* Gospel. But what is beyond doubt is that Jesus' first recorded demand upon men was not that they should worship Him or theologize about Him or build a Church around Him but that they should follow Him. And if it be retorted that the road of simple discipleship is barred to the modern Christian with his increasing knowledge and awareness of the complexity of his time, then I do not see how contemporary theology is going to re-open it. If Jesus' warning and promise, 'Inasmuch as you have done it unto the least of these, you have done it to me', does not sting us, stir us and get us on the move, then all the explanations of that verse by Biblical commentators and theologians are unlikely to do the trick.

Our obsession for matching complexity with complexity is part of the sickness of the Church. Having conceded the complexity of the world in which we live, intellectual respectability seems to demand that *our* solutions should be at least as complicated as *its* problems. 'Let's add our fog to your fog,' we say to the world, 'then we will both see twice as clearly!'

Do we really find it hard to understand why Albert Schweitzer, after two decades of rumination in the fields of theology and philosophy decided to become a doctor in Africa, so that he could do good without having to *say* anything?

The genius of Jesus was that He offered simple but costly solutions to complex problems. When Captain Oates, dying, walked out into the Antarctic night in order to save Scott's already weakened party from having to carry him, he cut through complexities and short-circuited a long discussion on a problem whose every aspect presented an ethical dilemma. His solution was sublimely simple and infinitely costly.

Thank God for the Reinhold Niebuhrs of the Church who, from a commanding vision, can trace God's action through the complex events of our time. The most, however, the average Christian can hope to do is to take hold of the near edge of a great problem and act at some cost to himself. The Church is not a Think-Group, whose role is to duplicate or supplement the intellectual efforts of others. It is an Action-Corps daring to offer simple solutions to complex problems through the creative use of self-sacrifice.

We are prone, alas, to forget this insight and offer to the world that which has cost us nothing. In the late 1950's when Britain was preparing to explode her first hydrogen bomb in the Pacific, the Churches yelled bloody murder, passed frenzied resolutions, protesting, deploring, expressing grave concern etc. etc., and delegations of ecclesiastical dignitaries and political pundits waited on the Prime Minister to threaten and plead. But it was a 60-year-old Unitarian who quietly withdrew his life savings, bought a little boat and sailed it into the centre of the Test Area as his personal protest. Of course it was idiotic, irresponsible, quixotic of him, but his action commanded a queer sort of respect because he was prepared to lay his life on the line for what he believed.

And we comfortable, well-fed, well-housed soldiers of Jesus, having made our big speeches and rolled the rhetoric around our tongues went to our beds the night the Bomb went off, shaking our heads sadly at the turn of events and hoping that someone would listen next time. They didn't and they won't. For politicians understand this word game too. Resolutions and deputations don't frighten them. If anything gives them unease it is crazy little men who sail right into the heart of big issues in total disregard for their lives. Such men are dangerous. The rest of us could not be tamer.

Our current obsession with theology is, in some measure, a mechanism for putting up a smoke screen of issues between ourselves and actual people. We baulk, as prudent men will, at the cruel demands made upon our personal resources of love and compassion by Jesus. By a kind of sleight of hand we transfer our awareness of human agony from our hearts to our heads and conceptualize the whole thing. Then we dissect and pronounce upon it, push our papers back into our brief cases and dash off to the next meeting where pre-packaged concern will be required of us.

I have before me the current issue of the *New Christian* in which the General Secretary of the British Council of Churches, Dr Kenneth Sansbury, reported on the Crete meeting of the Central Committee of the World Council of Churches. One paragraph runs as follows: 'The Central Committee reiterated what it had already said about Viet Nam, called for full religious liberty in Spain and offered the services of a mediator in Nigeria. It expressed serious concern over the world's food gap and protested against racial discrimination.' It is little wonder that the Church has almost ceased to be the target of satirical comedians. Not even the sharpest wit amongst them can parody us as effectively as we parody ourselves. But the image conjured up by that extraordinary paragraph ought to have been worth five minutes of the 'Frost Report' – this august body of men, trotting metaphorically round the world expressing concern at this, grave concern at that and very grave concern at something else.

Their sentiments were, I am sure, genuine. But it was that old word game again. We are vitally concerned about human suffering because we keep on and on and on saying so. But as a bed-rock Christian operation, it is all phoney, and the world knows it is phoney by simple logic. No human beings, even princes of the Church, have got that much compassion in them to pour out. They might look Nigeria in the face, glance at Viet Nam and shudder, but long before they reached the problem of world hunger they would be drained,

22

voiceless and broken. And those good men would have adjourned that meeting, greyer at the temples, utterly aghast at the enormity of what they had seen.

But so long as we need only wrestle with *issues*, our range is unlimited. We can tut-tut our way into, through and out of every problem on the entire globe, demands of the Agenda and tea-breaks permitting.

I write not in anger but in contrition, for I too have played that particular word game. I have been responsible for more than my fair share of pious resolutions, only one of which, demanding majority rule in what was then Northern Rhodesia, really cost me anything personally. For the rest, like Hans Andersen's little tailor, I have killed as many as seven or eight political issues with one blow in a single session of the Methodist Conference, merely by raising my hand dutifully at the appropriate moment.

We might feel a little cleaner, even if exposed as honest reactionaries, if we told the truth about this Resolution business. The overwhelming part of our time in Church assemblies and conferences is concerned solely with domestic matters, and that's how our administrators like it, but we have this thing about relevance and don't feel quite comfortable unless we have taken the odd peep outside the Church door. So our professional resolution writers, one eye on the morning paper, get to work, we vote, then pass on to the next business. 'We've ten minutes before the Devotional Session,' said the Secretary of the Methodist Conference at its 1967 meeting, 'we'll take the Resolution on Rhodesia!' So for the statutory ten minutes we beat the air with perfervid oratory, then consign an area of the world from which the Third (and final) War is likely to burst forth to the oblivion of our Minutes and get on with the main business of the Conference, spending hours tinkering with our structures and fencing with one another about Church Union. The Church has spoken about a contemporary issue. That's about it. We have spoken. But we don't sleep any the worse that night for our brief dalliance with Rhodesia or Viet Nam or the population explosion. Nor do those hapless millions about whose fate we sonorously pronounce, sleep any easier for knowing that we have spared them the odd ten minutes on a crowded agenda – 'We servants of Jesus Christ are with you in your agony . . . well, not exactly with you, but you know what we mean!' They know what we mean, all right. That's why we can't sell most of them institutional religion at any price.

Perhaps the way of Jesus – costly personal involvement in human suffering – is not always possible. Perhaps there are some problems about which we can do nothing practically. Then we should speak only with greatest reluctance. For our advice is of marginal value. It is the moral force of our willingness to out-sacrifice everyone else in the field that alone gives us the right to speak. In religion, as in roulette, if you have no money to put down, you must leave the game.

Because we are citizens of one world, moralizing, even at a distance, may have some value in symbolizing the responsibility of all mankind towards any part of it and in focusing our prayers. But it is interesting that there is no record of Jesus having made a moral judgement about anyone or any issue beyond the range of His possible physical presence. He was always on hand, open to the pointed finger of anyone who cared to challenge Him, to act out His words.

Having been critical of one aspect of the World

Council of Churches' activity, it would be churlish not to acknowledge the great work being done through its agencies to alleviate human suffering. Its very effectiveness points the moral that united action by Christians is more easily achieved when they form the kind of service agency that the whole Church was intended to be, and grapple with concrete human need rather than with each other in squabbles about dogma. Common acceptance of the Lordship of Christ is the sufficient theological motivation. In the front line, it is enough to know that someone is on your side; regimental competitiveness is a luxury of the base.

# *Two*

THERE are, in our day, Biblical scholars like William Barclay whose great learning is deployed in making Jesus plain to ordinary men and women and theologians who have a prophetic gift for cutting through complexities and confronting us with God's demand in words winged with fire. But the Church has had long experience in dealing with her prophets. She damns them to premature immortality and delivers them up into the hands of the academic theologians. Hence, the stabbing writings of Bonhoeffer are buried under a mass of writings about the writings of Bonhoeffer, and the Bishop of Woolwich, who gave a sense of liberation to thousands of ordinary Christians, is now the subject of learned works with titles such as *The Doctrine of the Church in the Writings of the Bishop of Woolwich*. We take the sting out of their words by analysing instead of acting upon them.

Such men suffer the fate of those fleas of Alexander Pope which had lesser fleas upon their backs to bite them – their knifing insights are blunted by being passed through the interpretive filters of lesser minds. The moment the focus of their words is switched from the street corner or the market place to the theological seminar and university lecture room they are doomed. We deal with them the way an oyster deals with an irritating grain of sand in its innards – cover them with pearl and consign them to the Theological Hall of Fame. It is only a matter of time before *Letters and Papers from Prison* and *Honest to God* will rest alongside Calvin's *Institutes* and Barth's *Commentary on Romans*, venerated by all and read only by those looking for a suitable Ph.D. subject. And the bell they tolled is muted from the clang of a tocsin to the tinkle of a vesper call.

That is the judgement upon us. We argue about such prophets, analyse and classify them, divide up into pressure groups for and against them, *but we do not do what they say*. Here, surely, lies the difference between live and dead theology. Live theology can be directly applied to everyday life. Dead theology paralyses action by its sheer volume, its obscurity and its concern for things so remote from the lives of ordinary men that they dismiss Christianity as a hobby for the clever rather than embrace it as a life that can be lived out in their little patch.

The Gospel of John says that he who *does* the truth comes to the light. It is a curious phrase but it puts the whole thing in perspective. The Gospel can never be anything other than simple, whatever some purveyors of cold wisdom in the theological schools may say, because it is meant to be *done*. Much modern theology fails us at this point. It offers no level from which to apply pressure upon the world and *move* something.

Certainly we should be grateful for the painstaking work of scholars who have delivered into our hands as pure a text of the Gospel as we are ever likely to have.

But much of the tinkering with tiny details of Christian origins and the exploration of historical by-paths evokes the cry of the homeless family, fuming as they watch the interior decorator paint delicate patterns on the ceiling: 'For God's sake, we'll do without the fancy bits! When can we move in?'

It is this leisureliness of theological scholarship that baffles ordinary men. There is no sense of terrible urgency, no consciousness of an unrepeatable opportunity. The drama of the Gospel stirs men to expect the strident cry 'Act now or all is lost!'; instead they are treated to a cultivated drawl 'Don't get excited! This is a tentative contribution to the debate!' Many theologians seem to spend their time waiting for Godot, the Big Brain who will put together all the tiny pieces they have isolated so lovingly. Only then can the Church act with reasonable certainty. They function like the old barber-surgeon's apprentice who makes practice incisions in the patient, assuring him all the time that this is not the real operation; the master is on his way to do that. But the patient bleeds to death all the same.

Dr Alec Vidler, writing the Introduction to that volume *Soundings*, says: 'The authors of this volume of essays cannot persuade themselves that the time is ripe for major works of theological construction or reconstruction. It is a time for ploughing and not reaping; or to use the metaphor we have chosen for our title, it is a time for making soundings, not charts or maps. If this be so, we do not have to apologize for inability to do what we hope will be possible in a future generation. We can best serve the cause of the truth and of the Church by candidly confessing where our perplexities lie, and not making claims which, so far as we can see, theologians are not at present in a position to justify.'

Such modesty is disarming. But it does little to cushion the reader against the shock of finding out that theology has changed its role from reflecting upon the certainties of faith to sharing the perplexities of doubt. And it prompts a question. What about the poor mutt who takes the contents of that book seriously and decides that much of what he previously believed is erroneous? What does he do about his faith in the interim until someone decides that the time *is* ripe for theological reconstruction? Having accepted the invitation to leave a sinking ship, he finds himself on one that won't float. He is left with two alternatives. He can either go on believing truths that his academic betters assure him are false or he can adopt a Yoga-like immobility and freeze, hoping the theologians will revive him when they've got the show on the road again.

It is little wonder that some of the finest Christian service of our day is being done by men and women who have sworn an oath never to set foot in a religious bookshop or otherwise inhale the theological miasma. They struggle along as best they can using a combination of the New Testament and plain common sense.

When we apply the test of *doing the truth* to our heated theological controversies we are exposed as Don Quixotes tilting at windmills and not as Luthers crying 'Here I stand!' And all our numerous theological groupings are reduced to a simple two – there are those who put their theology into action and those who don't. The theology in question may require the theoretical superstructure of Karl Barth's *Church Dogmatics* or may be simple Bible-religion. But it is put to work. It is truth that is *done*.

My grandstand view of the martyrdom of the Church in the Congo Counter-revolution taught me to distrust those conventional labels we pin on our fellow Christians. Over three hundred missionaries, mostly Roman Catholics and extreme fundamentalists, were killed. They not only bled the same way but whether they died clutching crucifixes or Schofield Reference Bibles they died for the same reason and the same Lord.

When the chips were down in that tragic mess, men and women stood revealed for what they were, their theological labels abandoned with the rest of their possessions. Some theological radicals, fond of booming about *relevance* and *involvement* were not to be found. Their presence was urgently needed elsewhere. It was often Bible-punching conservatives who believed literally in Adam and Eve and damned drinkers and smokers and swearers to hell who stood up to be counted. Your theology, fancy or plain, is what you are when the talking stops and the action starts.

That phrase *Revolutionary Christianity* is fashionable. But what it describes is more often a way of talking than a way of walking. It is revolution at the level of argument rather than action. We take daring liberties with the Christianity of the Creeds and the traditional ideas about God. We go into the fray, armed to rend an Altizer or Woolwich apart or defend them to the death. We sup the heady wine of controversy and nail our colours to the mast – mixing our metaphors in the excitement! The Church, we cry, is in ferment. She has bestirred herself out of her defensive positions and is on the march! And so she is – on the march to the nearest bookshop or theological lecture room or *avant garde* church to expose herself to the latest hail of verbal or paper missiles.

This is not revolution. It has more in common with the frenzied scratching of a dog to rid itself of fleas than an epic march on the Bastille or the Winter Palace. Revolutionary Christianity is so uncomplicated in comparison that it is almost embarrassing to have to put it into words. It is simply doing costly things for Jesus' sake.

For the life of me I cannot see why a world which has rejected the God of traditional theology should find Woolwich's or Tillich's *God Beyond God* any more interesting. For this is really exchanging the theological word-game for the word-game of the philosophers, and both are intellectual pastimes whose devotees are probably less numerous than *Times* crossword fans though drawn from the same corners of our society. The judgement upon us is not that we have failed to bring our theology into line with the best modern thought, though that may be true, but that we do not act to the limit of the theology we already have.

Nothing we *say* is going to make much of a dent in the hard crust of modern society, for we are just one amongst many firms of word merchants peddling our wares. It is not without significance that the embargo on Western missionaries entering certain ex-colonial territories admits of only two exceptions – Quakers and the Salvation Army – two Action Corps which are no great shakes at theology, both content to throw in their weight in practical service over central areas of human need. And a hard-bitten world is too impressed with their sacrifice to sneer at their simplicity.

Let me introduce you to one of the revolutionaries of the modern Church. He is a missionary with an awesome lack of gifts and graces, the kind of man whose presence in the ministry is explained by the assumption that he must have been a delicate child. To him, if the word signified anything, *Bultmann* would be the name of a race horse. During the Lumpa War which ravaged Zambia's Northern Province in the summer of 1964, he spent two weeks of nights sleeping in a deserted village from which all the people had fled, fearing a Lumpa attack. Every night he sat, scared to death, alone in a little hut, jumping at every sound, in order to encourage the villagers to come out of the bush and return to a normal life. He is still around Zambia, boring congregations with his inadequate preaching, and would be horrified if anyone suggested that he was one of the revolutionaries of the Faith, for he likes to call himself a conservative.

To those who know him, he is a man of commanding authority. For when the chips were down, he stood up to be counted. He lived to the limits of his restricted theology and did a costly thing for Jesus' sake. He typifies thousands of Christians whom the present theological ferment leaves high and dry. They cannot juggle philosophical concepts in their minds, nor if the truth were known, have they any great sense of the importance of dogma, which we professionals assure them is of such significance that Christians must be kept in separate pens to keep it pure. Their only hope of reaching the light is through a truth they can put into action.

It would be grossly unfair to the theological controversialists of our day to imply that they would not stand up to be counted in the limiting situation. I am sure they would, gladly. Dietrich Bonhoeffer is their patron saint. Had he lived, he would probably have revised or even abandoned the theological position for which he is now widely known. But speculation about the development of his thought is pointless. It is his witness which was absolute and beyond revision. Some

Christians, I among them, will remember him with gratitude not chiefly for *Letters and Papers from Prison*, but for another book whose title he spelled out in blood – *The Cost of Discipleship*. Yet his thoughts from the prison cell command an authority they might never have achieved in the university lecture room. They are the reflections of one doing the truth, at terrible cost.

Theological ferment is valuable when it makes great demands upon the mental processes of Christians but the Church's major problem is how to enlist their compassion. This is not an anti-intellectual remark. To talk of the simplicity of the Gospel is not to reduce it to a moronic Jesus-jingle. Its simplicity is its total lack of ambiguity, dead-ends and irrelevances. From whatever point in time or geography, out of whatever psychological type or social class you come within range of the Gospel, if you consent to open your ears to hear, you will be carried along irresistibly to a moment of truth that evokes from you the question of the rich young ruler 'What, then, must I do?' And you are told!

Being put through the wringer, whose upper and lower rollers are God's Mercy and Judgement, is bound to be as much a mind-stretching operation as anything else. But what is lacking in many worthwhile theological works of our time is that final chapter which sounds a prophetic 'Now, therefore, children of Israel . . .' – a phrase that always announces the point in God's arguments with His people when the crunch comes and they are put to the test of his practical demands.

The playwright, John Osborne, in the book *Declaration* has some bitter words about the Church's failure to make the connection between its theology and its action, though that is not how he would put it! Don't

3

be deluded by his shrillness. There is moral indignation woven into his words: 'Every day on the radio, in the press and on television, the Church hawked around its Jesus Figure like a vacuum cleaner, but nobody felt inclined to buy a machine that not only failed to beat, sweep and clean, but actually made a nice mess as well. It had JESUS written on the bag, but the bag contained only the air of another bunch of overpaid liars. When the Jesus jingles came on, most people simply switched off their responses automatically and waited for the next programme. They knew the people selling the product were themselves utterly incapable of making the damn thing *work*. They behaved exactly like the people selling something else, or who, better still, were selling nothing at all. Like so many other English Institutions, the Church was beginning to lose its comic value.'

No sales pitch will win over a man of that degree of articularity and cynicism. No polishing up of our patter using with-it jargon or fashionable philosophical terms will get under his guard, for words are his business too. Maybe nothing will. But maintaining a dignified silence in the face of such a vicious attack does not excuse us from making the vacuum cleaner *work*!

Theological radicalism is beyond most Christians. They have neither the head nor the stomach for it. And by this I do not mean that they are too dim to realize what is at stake. They realize, all right, which is why they cannot be coaxed into spending precious time and energy turning our theological treadmills. Moral radicalism, the willingness to do costly things for Jesus' sake, is not beyond them, provided their imaginations and consciences are fired and they are shown the truth they must do *by leaders who get alongside*

34

*them* and live through the experience with them.

You can lead a theological revolution from an Oxford College, a great pulpit or an Archbishop's palace but those revolutions that rock the world are led from the middle of the crowd. Karl Marx indeed changed the shape of the world from a desk in the Reading Room of the British Museum, but the world we have inherited from him sweeps contemptuously aside all forms of hierarchical leadership, both political and ecclesiastical. It is the first man through the barricades the people follow. The New Africa was carved out of colonial torpor by faceless men, without rank and precedence in society. They were marked out from their fellows by two simple qualities, the ability to feel more deeply and to absorb more punishment. Any true leadership the Church throws up in our day will need these two things whatever other gifts and graces we require of it.

Theologizing at a distance as a spur to action is out of the question in our world. Any new thinking will have to be done on the march. Such thinking is likely to be crude and as plain as a cheap suit, but it will be effective because it makes no pretentious claims and shapes itself into no elaborate systems. It will be the minimum necessary theological framework to support recognizably Christian action. And it is on the march that most Christians will fight their way through to a living faith. They are bewitched, bothered and bewildered by the attempts of contemporary theologians to tell them what they ought to believe, what they can believe, and what is no longer believable. They will hammer out their creed as they follow through a programme of humane action, either out of the belief that they are doing the will of Jesus or if they cannot say even that much, by doing costly things any way as the response of compassion to raw human need – relying on that Biblical promise that he who loves is born of God and knows God.

Granted, such action-theology is unlikely to be extensive enough to make Church Union squabbles worthwhile, but then I honestly believe we can get by with a lot less theology provided the little we need is all used up. Doctrines, however venerable, which cannot be put into action in the work-a-day world can safely be left in the care of the technical theologians who will preserve them in an atmosphere as cold as a refrigerator.

The worship of men and women spending themselves in compassionate action would have an air more of desperation than formality. They would stagger into Church utterly drained of goodness, unable to face another day unless their numbed spirits were re-sensitized and their strength renewed. They would be too hoarse to sing, too stiff to kneel and too dog-tired to take in any long exhortations from the pulpit. They would await the reading of the Lesson with something akin to dread as God presented them with yet more impossible demands. Every false word in the service would stick out like a sore thumb and pretentiously ornate language would be heard no more. Instead, they would gasp out a simple litany exposing the horror and pain and misery they had shared, asking God to show them Jesus in it.

In this context, the most familiar truth would scorch. They would gulp the bread of Communion like starving men and reach out for the wine with the trembling hand of an alcoholic. What they knew about Crucifixion they would learn from the back streets of their town rather than the hymns of Charles Wesley. And they would not casually go through the motions of a ritual expectation of Resurrection on that first day of the week. There would be a heart-stopping suspense as the service progressed. Would they really find a Risen Lord at work in the heart of the tragic mess to which they would have to return? But would He accept a concrete deed as His due in place of a spiritualized devotion they could not affect?

The deadly formality of much of the Church's worship is at root a symptom of the drastic under-employment of Christians. The great liturgies of the Church evolved from the experiences of men who went in fear of their lives and huddled together for protection. To be 'sealed with Christ in His death' was not a pious phrase but a real possibility. Though archaic language may indeed be a barrier against communication, the main reason why many of the forms of worship we have inherited seem dead is that our experience is too miniscule to latch onto the reality of which they speak. We slop around in the great Offices of the Church like little girls in their mother's shoes or boys in father's trilby. Oxygen tents are not for those with insect bites.

Besides bringing worship to life, the subordination of theology to action might also release some of that store of intellectual and nervous energy at present dedicated to ecclesiastical blood-letting. Quarrels in an over-loaded life boat wallowing in shark-infested seas could hardly be less useful or dignified than the bad temper we exhibit when we hound our fellow Christians who do not worship or witness our way. I am not now thinking of theological dialogue or even healthy, robust controversy but a darker, more sinister thing that drives us to attempt to undermine another man's

37

witness in the interests of what we miscall the truth.

Let it be so much as whispered that Billy Graham is *en route* for Britain to conduct an evangelical campaign and some of the best brains in the Church mobilize themselves to do a demolition job on him before he even sets foot off the boat at Southampton. The air is thick with accusations and counter accusations and any apparent set-back in his fortunes is greeted with jubilation. Other sectors of the Church showed the same malicious and destructive spirit following the publication of *Honest to God*. A Church which can afford to pour that much energy down the sewer has too much time on its hands. And in the polluted atmosphere of clever malice that hangs over the Church at such times, our claim to offer a Gospel of Reconciliation rings as hollow as the sales-pitch of a bald-headed man selling hair restorer.

# *Three*

I SEEM to have strayed a long way from the little man with the shrunken belly who started all this. But I have not forgotten him, nor ever could. As a statistic he is eminently forgettable. As a fiery visitation from God he has limitless capacity to stab the conscience awake. My digression was necessary in order to convince myself that I am totally without excuse; that pressure of Church business or duty of worship or welfare of my well-fed flock cannot be pleaded by way of mitigation. I had to remind myself that Christianity is humane action for Jesus' sake at cost to myself; that, and nothing much else of any significance. I had to remind myself what Christianity is because I have spoken and written and argued about it so much that I had quite forgotten, as a man has been known to forget his own name and address in a moment of crisis.

Two thousand years of Christian history were blown away by the faint sigh of that little man's last breath. It is pointless turning up the figures of the Methodist Relief Fund or Christian Aid. He died without knowing that Jesus cared for him, not in a sentimental, spiritua-

39

lized way, but by the offer ot a square meal. It just happened that none of Jesus' men were around to give it to him, so he died and Jesus died with him. And for one Christian at least the Church sinks into the limbo of those three long days, lifeless, leaderless and in mourning. Choose a Resurrection Hymn and the words would choke me. That is sheer lack of faith, of course. For we are taught that ours is the victory in spite of everything; that the Church moves like a mighty unbeatable army. But I have a feeling that the Church's invulnerability relates to outside attempts to destroy her. She is defenceless against self-mutilation. 'Yet again,' says Jesus, 'Yet again, must I go through this?' We certainly don't think He ought. For the murder of six million Jews possibly, or the slaughter of twelve million men in war, but hardly for a microscopic martyrdom like the death of one hungry little man. But He does. And the question is: when will He rise again?

This whole massive structure we call a Church with all its history, theology, worship and witness is a great pyramid on a point. It is meant to be brought to focus upon any one man's need. That is what all the singing and praying and Bishops and sacraments and preaching is about. It is about the paramount significance to God of a single human being's need. And if we fail in that one thing, we fail in everything.

It was a Hindu holy man, Vivanakanda, who said that he who suffers is God's representative. I doubt that Jesus would have argued with him. So God's chosen one visited the Church. He came attired not in the splendour of an Archbishop's robes or the well-cut suit of a Nonconformist prince, but in a pair of shorts and a ragged shirt, and his sceptre was an empty biro pen.

He came and found the Church empty. Full of people and activity and plans. But empty for him. For we did not see him. And we did not see him because his name is Legion, for there are many like him.

He came and passed on. He walked out through the paper walls of the Church and it is too late to call him back and offer him the chief seat at the feast. So we are left with the debris of a banquet and no guest of honour.

Our failure towards the little people of the earth is more than a lapse of simple charity for which sincere contrition can atone. When our Churches have crumbled and our vestments have rotted and the wind blows through the ruins of our ecclesiastical structures, all that will stand and have eternal significance are creative acts of compassion – the effectual signs of the presence of the Kingdom.

Because the Gospel is simple, the judgement is immediate. It awaits no historical summing up of all things. It can be put plainly and in first-person terms. I saw a starving man and there was no gnawing pain in my belly. I saw a hunchback and my own back did not ache. I watched a pathetic procession of refugees, being herded back and forth sleeplessly, and I slept well that night.

The theologians call it Identification and it is worth fifty pages in a reputable text book. It is easier to read the fifty pages than to feel one pang. Those of us concerned about the relevance of the Church spend our time trying to answer Bonhoeffer's question 'What is Christ in our day?' with learned papers instead of crusts of bread and are puzzled that we can reach no firm conclusions.

No Christian is without excuse for this drying up of the

springs of compassion but the judgement is the more terrible on those who are called or call themselves leaders of the Church. There is a lovely, or frightening, story in the Midrash about the call of Moses. In the translation by Edmund Fleg it runs as follows: 'One day a kid escaped from the flock. Moses hastened after it to a rocky place where he found it drinking at a spring. "Poor kid", he said to it, "Thou didst flee in order to drink? Surely thou art now full weary." He took it on his shoulder and brought it back to the flock. Then God said, "Since he hath had pity upon a poor kid, bearing it upon his shoulder to take upon him its weariness, then he will have pity upon my poor people."

'For God before entrusting the flocks of men to His Kings and prophets, entrusts to them, to try them, the least of the flocks of His beasts.'

Dare God trust His poor people to us? Indeed, does He trust them to us or has He made other arrangements? Is this possibly why our ringing calls for renewal and advance sound hollowly around our assemblies and conferences and echo back to mock us? Our failure has not been in matters of great moment. We can rise to the big occasion, beguiling men with our eloquence, moving them to laughter and tears. We are faithful stewards of the Church's resources and kindly fathers to her children. But was there somewhere, some time a decisive encounter with an unnoticed human being, whose need would have undammed those springs of compassion that solidify into cold wisdom with disuse, if only we had seen him? Did we wish him a polite good morning and hurry on our way about God's business, and as a consequence of that unremembered failure to ease another's pain forfeit the right to wear the proud apparel of the servants of Christ?

That 'sick' comedian, Lenny Bruce, who committed suicide at the turn of the year, cut to the heart of the matter in a single biting epigram. He said 'I know in my heart, by pure logic, that any man who claims to be a leader of the Church is a hustler if he has two suits in a world in which most people have none.'

Anyone in the house care to argue? We can comfort ourselves, if we will, with the knowledge that Bruce was banned from every public place of entertainment in the United States for obscenity and died virtually penniless. Does that reinforce our sense of virtue, or can we see that what he was describing is a greater obscenity than all the filth that poured from his mouth?

We are those who rise in our wrath at the prevalent use of four-letter words that are at worst mere evidence of tastelessness or verbal ineptitude. The real obscenity, which should stick in our throats and choke us, is what we have done in Christ's name to degrade that little man with a shrunken stomach with all our pious concern and carefully doled out charity and fervent prayer and passionate assurances that we intend to get around to his plight when we have put our own house in order.

Obscenity is a strong word, but I know no other so apt. Obscenity is the jewelled ring on a bishop's finger. It is the flash of my gold wrist watch from under the sleeve of my cassock as I throw dirt on the coffin of a man who died of starvation, murmuring, the while, the most asinine words in the English language – 'Since it has pleased Almighty God to take to himself our brother.' Obscenity is the cardinal who cries 'Murder!' when a woman aborts a piece of bloody tissue but keeps

43

silence or indeed gives his blessing whilst thousands of fully formed sons and daughters of women are incinerated in Viet Nam.

Obscenity is the sincere Methodist layman, pausing to eat a second cream bun from his well-laden Sunday tea table before penning an indignant letter to the *Methodist Recorder* about the evils of fermented communion wine. Obscenity is the scurryings hither and thither of us homburg-hatted clerics with our bulging brief cases and our crowded diaries, protesting that the reason for our frenzied activity is the desire to be Christ to that little man with the shrunken stomach.

Obscenity is our zealous begging of money off people and organizations who are more amenable to our blackmail than our message in order to restore our crumbling edifices or to build new ones which are materialized lies – for the reality of our spiritual life would fit neatly into a telephone booth.

Obscenity is all our concern for our ecclesiastical dignity that will not allow us to make fools of ourselves for Christ's sake, and our one-eye-on-the-audience posturings of piety and humility.

Obscenity is our bleat of pious hope in situations too tragic for tears and our graceless despair when men do a worthwhile thing without invoking our help.

Obscenity is the grotesque caricature we have made of Jesus as we drag Him through the streets on high days and holy days like the Hunchback of Notre Dame, wearing a crown that symbolizes not His Royalty but our power-hunger.

Obscenity is the skill with which we pull the wool over the eyes of simple men so that they reach up gratefully for bread that crumbles to dust in their hands.

Obscenity is the deadly ease with which I and all

ecclesiastical word-mongers can write of hungry little men when our hands ought to tremble and refuse to do our bidding.

Lord, have mercy upon us! The Church is incurably craven and hopelessly compromised and fit only to be trampled under the feet of men. And yet . . .

And yet . . . may this not be the greatest obscenity of all – to set myself over against the Church and apply the whip to her back to demonstrate that, unlike her, I am not beyond salvation? To attack the Church is to pick the easiest target in sight. Kick the world and it kicks back, but the Church appears to absorb limitless punishment with apparent passivity. When I attack the Church I can only get hurt by accident; by a sort of involuntary muscle spasm in reaction to my blow. And any domestic persecution I suffer at her hands only serves to add perverted zest to a frenzy reminiscent of the man who dug his mother-in-law's grave twelve feet deep because he liked to take pleasure in his work.

As a pastime, reviling the Church from the inside has much in common with kicking one's mother. It is aggression without consequences, a mock heroism that allows the strut of bravado secure from retaliation. And like all violent rejection of parents, it is in our moods of flaring anger that we look most like them – an expression in the eye, a tone in the voice gives us away – we are never more obviously their offspring than at the moment of declaring our independence. This is why the music hall parody of the parson sounds less ecclesiastical than an ex-son or daughter of the Church castigating her. Everything is there; the sanctimoniousness, the prophetic heat, the cold priestly righteousness, the pastoral concern for the betrayed millions. What could be more pious than taking one's stand for God against the Church?

Though I would like to call myself a true rebel, I cannot cut myself free from the Church. This is not only because I have a personal share of responsibility for her failures and so must stand the racket, but also because it was through the cracked and distorting mirror of the Church that I first saw the One by whose side I seek to take my stand in the life of the world. And that image haunts me. Happy are those who are open to a new manifestation of Jesus in the life of the world because they have not lived with the Church's Jesus, had their minds moulded by a strait-jacket of dogma and their souls nourished on a diet of Word and Sacrament. They are free. We are captives of the Church. She is an incubus with which we must live, just as Jesus must live with the incubus of ourselves.

It is the humiliation of the Church that puts the strongest grip on us. We cannot follow Christ's command to feed the hungry and ignore the fact that she too, is famished. We cannot seek in Jesus' name to heal the sick and turn a blind eye to her diseases. We cannot try to raise the dead and be immune to the stench that rises from her mortification. For it is both bad theology and poor observation to suggest that the Church has no need of the Gospel.

Our strident and bitter denunciations of the Church leave no serious wound. The most devastating judgement of the Church comes from the man who, with exquisite politeness, as though raising his hat to a lady, walks quietly out without a cross word or murmur of disappointment and gets on with the business of living without her, a tolerant but utterly unapproachable neighbour. All our anguished howls at the Church's callowness and shortcomings are really protestations of loyalty to a Church that could exist and does exist somewhere. They scream the necessity, *for us*, of the Church.

There are many reasons why I cannot extricate myself from the Church. For one thing, I have persuaded too many others to follow me through her doors, to eat at her table and put their destiny in her keeping. Can you invite refugees to take shelter in your home and then burn it down round them because in a moment of disillusionment the architecture seems dismal?

Deeper yet is the smart of knowing that the only failure of the Church that signifies is my own. Henry Miller, a novelist noted more for the vigour of his prose than its polish, says of the world that it is a mirror of ourselves, and adds, 'If it is something to make one puke, why then, puke, me lads, it's your own sick mugs you're looking at!' For *world* read *Church* and it would be just as true. I can only talk of the Church as a great pyramid brought to a focus at the point of any one man's need if I am also to admit that I personally am not safely swallowed up in the body of it but fully exposed at its extremity. And when a blunt pencil will not write, sharpening the point is the first thing to do whatever else may be needed.

Abraham Lincoln's advice to a gang of train robbers that hanging together was the best way of avoiding hanging separately applies to the corporate responsibility of the total Christian fellowship. But it is little comfort to us. Jesus has a way of elbowing through the crowd and testing His Church by casual encounters, as a man will test a box of fruit by picking one up at random. So, like Tolstoy's madman, the Christian rebel cries 'I am running away from something dreadful and cannot escape it. I am always with myself and it is I who am my tormentor.' All disillusionment with the Church is, at root, an expression of self-disgust.

My hopeless involvement with the Church has nothing to do with her infallibility, for she obviously has none. Nor is it because in Paul's phrase she is the Body of Christ – a concept of the Church productive of most world-denying heresies with its implication that mankind is divided into two realms, one where Jesus is present with special intensity and another from which He is more or less absent unless we take Him there. The inevitability of the Church is an organic fact. The reality of the Church has been burnt into my soul. I am like the former inmate of the concentration camp whose number is indelibly tattooed on his wrist so that he is marked for life.

Some day, the genetical biologist will explain this strange thing, possibly by proving that some people have a religion-chromosome amongst the chromosomes that determine aspects of their personalities from their sex to the colour of their eyes. If he does isolate such a religion-chromosome, it may explain why we can preach at some men until we are blue in the face but they never see the light. Maybe they haven't got that genetical itch and are religion-deaf as others are tone-deaf or colour blind. And the doctrine of Predestination the Church has almost abandoned may have to be looked at again in the light not of the Bible but of genetics. In the meantime, the Church and I seem to have concluded a pact of mutual hindrance. She is the ball and chain round my leg; I am the handcuffs on her wrists.

Then, there is that other thing – the matter of a

covenant from which only death will release us, binding us in a continual act of obedience to Jesus. This is not an arrangement that can be terminated when we no longer feel satisfaction or get intellectual stimulus out of the Christian life. It is a willingness to be burned to death or bored to death for Jesus' sake, and who, in the context of the modern Church, can doubt that the latter is the more terrible fate? This is in no sense a contract agreed between two equals to walk together for as long as their company is congenial. There is about it more of the dumb obedience of the ox than the joyful acquiescence of the free agent. It is a burden shouldered, often against our better judgement, out of a recognition that there must be a necessary curb upon a proud spirit that would otherwise expand until it committed the ultimate sin and filled the centre of the universe. There is a level of existence where sheer animal-like *submission* to someone is necessary to prevent our pride confronting the religion of God become Man with another: that of Man become God. And if we are going to put ourselves unconditionally at anyone's mercy, whom can we trust but Jesus?

If I break that covenant, there is no reason why the world should trust me to pay my gas bill or keep my garden tidy or empty my dust bin. Jesus has something to say about the reliance that can be placed upon those who show fidelity in small things. He tactfully refrains from sketching the fate of those who prove faithless in large things. But His silence is eloquent.

This idea of the Christian life as a life-long covenant of obedience to Jesus is both too simple and too hard to be given much house-room in a world where consumer-satisfaction is the test of everything; where we can always get our money back if we are not pleased with what we have bought. But 'foolishness to the Greeks' is an understatement of the intellectually indefensible things this covenant drives us to do.

For example. Politically, in an age of nationalism, Christian missions are hopelessly compromised. Yet Jesus said 'Go, preach the Gospel to all nations.' It is a command, and we have no option but to obey. Psychologically, preaching is a discredited method of communicating the truth, but we have been commanded to 'Proclaim the Lord's Death till He come', so we have got to do it. Viewed sociologically, the Christian community does not match up to our confident claims, but we must maintain our sacramental existence because we have been commanded to do thus and thus 'in remembrance of Me.' And we must obey.

This is not a cheerful note to strike in a day when the Church is struggling madly to attract new recruits, and if its full implications were realized our membership losses would rise still more steeply. Yet it is an anchor, that covenant, that might keep a man within the Church when so many things she does seem calculated to drive him out in disgust.

Let me confess it. I am afraid of the Church. I don't know whether I fear her most when she appears as a prince to command me or as a beggar to cajole me. I hate her power yet cannot live with her indecision. I fear her eloquence almost as much as the eloquence she stirs up in me. I fear both the wealth that makes her a multi-million pound industry and the poverty that has her protesting her inability to spare a trifling sum for a daring experiment or a new work. I am afraid of her bewildering changes of mood from senility to adolescence, and the capriciousness that calls me to a life of sacrifice and then keeps me in comfort.

Most of all I fear that cock-sureness with which the Church grants me the freedom to make my own discovery of the meaning of Jesus and then with unholy glee proves that my hard won insight is some old heresy she shrugged off centuries before.

There are some species of fear that can be overcome by avoiding the occasions that call them out – riding in lifts, standing on top of high buildings, crawling through dark tunnels. But a Christian must live with his fear of the Church for the same reason a neurotic fish must live with its fear of water.

And it is the inevitability of the Church *for me* that has me joining the rest of the radicals in chasing the great theological red herring of our time – the search for ways of achieving a New Reformation. Much of the thinking, planning and strategy collectively known by this term, though its target is the world, is little more than a desperate attempt to ensure the survival of the Church. An American layman, William Robert Miller, analysing the general trend of the Bishop of Woolwich's thought, writes in the Spring, 1967, issue of *The American Scholar*: 'Robinson may not have intended it so, but his plea for a new reformation turns out to be an appeal to the church to lift itself by its own boot-straps, to achieve a more intelligent and stream-lined orthodoxy through better use of its extant resources. Nothing basic is risked: churchmen will become better Christians by using better methods; they will be kept in the church by undertaking to serve those outside it; and the church will prosper because the walls come down to give it access to the world . . . it will all sound different, one will sing the tune to a new beat and even improvise on it, but underneath the atonality it is still "Onward Christian Soldiers". One will make

Christianity secular, existential, humanistic, dialectical even atheistic, but it will still be somehow doctrinally untransformed and, above all, churchly. . . .'

Because such staggering claims are made for the Church in the body of our dogma (though we are careful to hedge our bets by conceding that in practice she often fails to live up to what she really is) we project her inevitability *for us* into a claim that she ought to be inevitable for everyman. And when the masses show a bland disregard for their churchly destiny, whereas in the centuries of our dominance we would have ascribed this to *their* sinfulness, in the century of our humiliation we take the rap ourselves for *our* failure to be truly the Church. Yet there is no reason to assume that we should have even marginally more appeal if we did put our house in order. The chances are that our numbers would dwindle still further.

Only Jesus is inevitable in this time or any other. The Church, viewed coldly in isolation from our claims for her, is nothing more than an experiment in applied Christianity based upon a certain way of looking at and reacting to Jesus. But we have no monopoly of Him. We say this all the time, of course, but we still behave as though we had. This One who 'is in all, through all and over all' is much bigger than that system of belief and practice we call Christianity. We in the Church follow the priest's Jesus and name Him as the One who is forever Christ, Lord and Saviour. But many more, not of our number, follow the prophet's Jesus who is known by many names or none. They stand for Him by doing the things He did. They form themselves into no organizations, though they will be found in many, they make no dogmatic claims, but in so far as they identify themselves with the lost, or heal or teach or prophesy or suffer for men, they are of Jesus and He is in them.

These, too, represent an experiment in applied Christianity. And no professor of comparative religion or intellectual observer can judge whether their way is better than ours. There is only one reliable judge. It is the little man with the shrunken belly. For he knows the shape and taste of bread. And he knows the bread he can safely swallow and that bread attached to a string by which he is yanked into the Church the moment he takes the bait.

Jesus saves him by feeding him, not by dying on a cross for him. That little man will have watched with hooded eyes thousands of his own kind, men, women and children, die deaths more lingering than crucifixion. There is no emotional appeal to him in that story. He has exhausted every sensation. It is the well-fed Westerner, protected from pain by science and technology, who is moved by the account of that violent death. But a piece of bread is a transformation of the little man's fortunes as dramatic as resurrection. It is Resurrection. He has been snatched out of the pit of death. The full Gospel has been expressed in the outstretched hand of another human being with a piece of bread in it. The label on it – compliments of the Christian Church, of the Communist Party, of Oxfam, of UNRRA – adds nothing either to its protein value or its theological significance. The whole saving work of Jesus is in the concrete deed. Whether the little man responds by singing 'Praise my soul the King of Heaven', the Red Flag or the 'Star Spangled Banner' is of little importance. He has been given life, with no strings attached. He has been transformed from a scratching animal into a man. He has, in short, been saved.

53

The distinctive contribution of the Church's experiment in applied Christianity is her ability to identify the One whom others follow anonymously. . . . 'What therefore you worship as unknown, this I proclaim to you' . . . in the words of Paul in the Areopagus. The Church must be inevitable for *someone* so that as a Community of Faith she can guard the historical record of the acts and words of Jesus. But knowledge of the source of bread is not the same as feeding the hungry. Indeed, does not Jesus specifically point out that the ability to name Him is of secondary importance? The blessed are not those who say Lord, Lord, but those who do what He commands. So the unchurched masses are unlikely to join our experiment in applied Christianity for the same reason that slum dwellers are unlikely to make the experiment of eating at the Savoy. The food would be too rich and the bill too heavy.

The official body of dogma puts such awe-inspiring labels upon the Church that we dare not use it for any purpose so mundane as an experimental laboratory of the Kingdom of God. The titles of our *alma mater* are so impressive that we must not appear before the world as anything less than absolute authorities. Our truth is a special kind of truth. Our compassion has a distinctive flavour. Any little man we succeed in feeding becomes, by virtue of that fact, different from little men that others feed. We are so conscious of our special destiny that we feel regretfully unable to throw in our weight with the other passengers bailing water out of the sinking boat. For we are the world authorities on water and to devote our skills to such a rough and ready task might cloud our judgement about the fundamental significance of water as opposed to any particular

54

sloppy manifestation of it. And anyway, as professionals we do not work happily alongside amateurs about whose true understanding of water we are doubtful. As the boat sinks slowly beneath the waves, we are heard to cry, 'We told you so!'

To deny any absolute claims to the Church and argue that the role of the Christian is to stand un-differentiated in the ranks of those vitally concerned about their fellow men, is to be accused of confusing Christianity with humanism. 'How does your behaviour differ from that of the humanist?' the orthodox ask, as though that disposed of the issue. The answer in my case is simple. Far from there being an over-plus of goodness I as a Christian can demonstrate which is beyond the best efforts of the humanist, my problem is that I need Christ in order to enable me to catch up with the humanist, let alone outstrip him. By nature, I do not happen to have what it takes to be a humanist. I have neither the courage nor the goodness. Only by doggedly following the will of Jesus am I fit even to lick the humanist's boots. That searching question of Jesus to His disciples 'What do you more than the rest?' would be rephrased in our day to 'Why do you not do as much as the rest?'

The plight of mankind is so desperate that the im-portant thing is to get the job done without worrying too much about who gets the credit. If the writings of Mao Tse Tung or Bertrand Russell do for any man what the words of Jesus are meant to do for me – inspire to costly humane action, then it is not for me to damn him with faint praise and claim that he would do even better if he were a Christian. If by that is meant 'within the ranks of the Church', it is almost certainly untrue. And in so far as he is alleviating the suffering of men, he is already sharing the Ministry of Jesus, whatever membership card he carries in his pocket. Only Jesus knows His own. Suppose He divides the Saved from the Lost not according to our elaborate schemes of Salvation but by the simple expedient of asking the little man with the shrunken stomach who did him good?

Because we cannot deny that the Kingdom of God is the ultimate goal and the Church a mere part of the scaffolding, we have got to take seriously the fact that most of Jesus' images of the Kingdom imply anonymity and imperceptibility. The Kingdom is present in the salt that gives tang to the food, the leaven that ferments the dough, the seed that grows secretly. Each operates by being swallowed up without trace in the whole substance of life. The erection of ecclesiastical fences in order to distinguish between those who are of Jesus and those who are not is one of the least rewarding occupations in the Kingdom, and introduces every conceivable kind of irrelevance. Everything boils down to the fate of that little man. It may be a matter for argument whether the bare act of giving him bread qualifies someone else for citizenship in the Kingdom of God. But it is beyond argument that I exclude myself from the Kingdom if I see his need and fail to feed him.

# *Four*

THE little man with the shrunken stomach is a prophetic sign. He tells us what is in our future. For the forces being generated by the hunger of people like him will shape the world in the next fifty years. Nothing and no one will escape from the blast of that hot breath. The whole inhabited earth will be contorted between the hammer of the Have Nots and the anvil of the Haves. Political ideologies, economic structures, social classes will reflect the image of hungry Man.

Two out of three human beings have not enough to eat at this moment, and the world is getting hungrier every day. Ponder these words from a recent Roman Catholic statement on world poverty: 'Within this narrow world of inescapable physical proximity, the small white Christian and Western minority are rich and grow richer. They make up not more than 20 per cent of the world's people. They consume some 75 per cent of the world's income. Moreover, they grow richer by not less than three per cent a year. In 1965, they *added* to their existing national incomes some seventy thousand million dollars – a figure which is considerably larger than the entire national income of all Latin America and twice as large as that of India or Africa. ....'

Those measured words sketch out the dimensions of a revolution that will convulse the planet and expose our present ferment in the Church as the gentle eccentricity of those who pick flowers on the slopes of a rumbling volcano. This is the great divide that no unity talk can bridge. Not between Christians and non-Christians, nor Catholics and Protestants, but between gluttons and paupers. And the judgement upon us is that we are an integral part of a gluttonous Church in a gluttonous society. We cannot speak to that other world because we are not even in it. We pursue our private obsessions whilst mankind is laid waste about us. Only the well-fed play at Church. The rest are too busy raking dust bins and garbage heaps for a morsel to feed their children.

It takes a man of rare courage to stand up in this world and proclaim the central importance to mankind of such matters as the meaning of episcopacy and the nature of the priesthood. It's all a game, my well-fed friends, a game played in a vast cemetery. And only those whose world ends at Dover will be disposed to dismiss that sentiment as melodrama.

The forces being generated by hunger are the Principalities and Powers of our time. The Devil stalks the earth tormenting, brutalizing and squeezing men dry, driving them to theft and murder and other nameless things in order to see their children fed. Anyone can buy their souls for the scraps we sweep into our kitchen bins. The Devil's name is Hunger. And God's name is Bread. That is the grand, all-embracing theological system within which the vast majority of mankind live. Exorcize that Devil and men might believe. Offer them a loaf of bread and they will fall down and worship.

There is one fatal flaw in all our worthy efforts to reform the Church and reconstruct Christian theology. It is the assumption that those to whom we speak will still be around in one week's time to continue the dialogue. Most contemporary theology is the product of men with alert minds and well-filled bellies. We take it for granted that those who hear us are in possession of the sinews of bare existence and have their wits about them. But those with these qualifications are the privileged few. What of the many whose minds are dulled by vitamin deficiency and whose survival turns upon a chance discovery in a rubbish heap or an unseasonable shower of rain or a visit from an Oxfam team or a sudden withering wind? What is the Gospel for them?

We in the west live in conditions of such unbelievable luxury that we cannot imagine what the Gospel sounds like to men on the other side of the Great Divide. Even when we make the effort to put it into their native tongue, they listen with a polite lack of interest because it is a fairy story about a strange world in which men eat regularly, and, because they are sure of that, can afford the luxury of a spiritual life.

As we set it out, the Gospel is concerned with what men do with their freedom of choice. The chronically hungry have no such freedom. They are conditioned like Pavlov's dogs who slaver at the mouth when a bell rings, their whole existence brought to a focus on a dish of food. 'Take no thought for the morrow!' implies that we can make meaningful choice between the world of insurance policies, social relief agencies, regular incomes, and a life of creative insecurity in reliance upon God's providence. The acceptance of uncertainty is a

Gospel virtue in the context of willing choice, but it has no significance whatever where choice is absent and precariousness is the very fabric of life.

The story of God's gift of manna in the desert to the Children of Israel is a heart-warming sermon subject for Christians hurrying home to their Sunday joint. Any missionary will tell you that it takes rather more explaining to those other peoples of the desert who see their children die with hunger before their eyes because no manna is forthcoming. Is it any wonder that many primitive languages contain no word for *God*? Nor need we be surprised if the hungry two-thirds of the world reject the God of metaphysics for the God of crude mechanics who makes water flow in the desert, whose footsteps are the roar of a tractor and whose voice is the clatter of machinery.

Christian apologetic is wont to claim that the flaw in Marxism is its insistence that man is a walking stomach. The laugh is on us. More and more poor nations will eagerly listen to the Gospel of Marx for that precise reason. It is your stomach not your soul that fills the universe when you can feel nothing but the pangs of hunger, hear nothing but the cries of starving children and see nothing but a world inhabited by skeletal figures scratching the ground.

In this bleak, arid world on the other side of the Great Divide, the servant of King Jesus rarely wears a clerical collar. More often the symbol of the presence of Christ is the grey tunic of the communist commissar, the toga of the nationalist leader or the over-sized cigar of the capitalist tycoon. These are Jesus to the people of that half-world because they meet men and women at the point of their most desperate need – bare life, not life under democracy or life in freedom or life to serve

God; just life. These atheistic Jesuses feed men. They regiment and coerce and bully and bribe and racketeer, but they give men bread. Bad Christian ethics, it will no doubt be retorted, for the question of means and ends is important. Why are these activists feeding hungry men? Isn't the grey-tunicked commissar feeding men in order to enslave them? Isn't the nationalist leader power-hungry, and the capitalist greedy?

Probably. But it doesn't matter. It is God's will that these little people should live and Jesus is the one who feeds them, *for whatever motive*, laudable or sinister. In *Christ and Methodism*, a book that packs more hard sense into a hundred pages than most theological works achieve in five times that compass, John Vincent writes: 'God has a *will*, a concrete, particular, if essentially hidden, will, which must be obeyed, and which is being obeyed not simply by those who intend to do so, but by all who in fact do so.

'The parable of the two sons is an obvious instance of this (Matt. 21, 28-31). The son who refuses God's claim, but then in fact grudgingly does what is required, is preferred to the son who honours the father in word, but never does what is required. It is the task, not the word, which is decisive. It is the deed, not the motive, which matters. It is whether somehow or other God gets His will done which is important, not whether we do it from love or reluctance.'

At the raw levels of life, which is where the majority of the world's population eke out a miserable existence, not only are distinctions between branches of the Christian Church of no significance but also distinctions between Christianity and Communism, humanism and nationalism, and any other 'isms' you care to name. The only distinction that matters is between those who eat as a right and those who must fight to eat. The only unity talk that is real is concerned with bridging that gap.

It is an illusion of the well-fed Westerner that there is a basic ethical distinction between living a regimented life in which you are fed, and enjoying the democratic freedoms in a society where your next meal is problematical. Some choice! Let the Christian ethics expert conjure with the problem of how a mother decides which of her children must starve to death in order that she can save some of them. She will sell her soul to the Devil or her body to the man next door to avoid making that choice. This is the *real* world, a world to which most of our proclamation and protestation is as irrelevant as good advice on how to set the dinner table tastefully and lay out the knives and forks in their correct order. For our theology takes *life* for granted instead of treating it as an open question.

The Moment of Truth will come some time in A.D. 2330. That is not my personal calculation of the likely date of Our Lord's Triumphal Return. It is the year, according to demographers, that the world's population will exactly equal the number of square yards on the earth's land surface. One Man, One Square Yard! will be the political slogan of the day. But long before that doomful time, we in the West will feel the jostle and press of those hungry hordes. Our time is up; theirs is beginning.

Against this sombre backdrop our current concerns have the aspect of a dying man manicuring his toe nails. No adjustments to our ecclesiastical structures can hide the terrible truth that our Church is immovably fixed on the wrong side of the barricades in the revolution of our time. And our Church is dying; slowly, gracefully dying. I know it is fashionable to use the image of a dying Church in our rhetoric and preaching to stir the faithful and give them a sense of urgency. I am not talking rhetoric but statistics. The Church of the Well-Fed that offers a well-nourished Jesus to congregations of good trencher-men is dying because it speaks to a constituency which is visibly shrinking. In the next 25 years, the population of the world will double, and for every bonny, healthy child born on our side of the barricade, ninety-nine skinny ones will pop up on the other side, far beyond the range of our evangelism. We are as much at one with our world and time as Irish landlords in the Great Famine.

It may be claimed that the Church is on *both* sides of the barricades, so that there is no wrong side; that our role is to offer the Gospel equally to a rich minority and a poor majority. We try to stand astride the Great Divide. At the level of argument that is true. Yet such judiciousness and careful balancing of claims and commitments betrays our pre-revolutionary orientation. For there is no middle ground in a revolution. You either charge with the crowd or walk to the guillotine. The *wrong* side of the barricade is the one where Christians, of all men, find themselves protecting what they have from those who have nothing. The *wrong* side is where those gather to whose advantage it is to resist revolution.

Jesus is on the other side of that barricade. Of that there cannot be a shadow of doubt, because He is a Revolutionary. And I am not using that term as a preacher's cliché for a man who did and said daring things, but in its technical sense. He is a Revolutionary because He stood for the radical discontinuity between the past and the future. He offered men no hope that they could build carefully and slowly upon what had gone before. The most fatuous words in the New Testament are those of Pilate: 'I can find no fault with this Man.' Whatever Pilate's ultimate fate, he deserved to be sacked for sheer stupidity. As a matter not of Atonement theory but political reality Jesus deserved to die, as many a man has died before and since, for taking a hatchet to the life-line of society, the slow, responsible shaping of the future from the past. His way was the way of political and social chaos, and society is entitled to protect itself against those who bring chaos in their wake.

Those hungry hordes too, will bring chaos in their wake. And we will be forced, in the interests of good order and stability and decency to resist them. By so doing, we shall be resisting Jesus the Chaos-Bringer. Yet we have no more option about resisting Him than had good honest Jews in the days of His flesh, concerned for the stability of their society. Because the logical consequence of all Jesus did and said is chaos, only those with nothing to lose can really follow Him for they alone have no fear of chaos. Certainly those with much to lose can accept Him as Personal Saviour at the cost of some personal sacrifice, but as the Bringer of the New Era only the mad or utterly desperate can follow Him.

We know Jesus is on the other side of that barricade because we know He is the One who by definition puts Himself outside every barrier, frontier and fence we choose to erect in order to safeguard what is our own, or even what we think is His. This is surely another reason why it is foolish to make absolute claims for the Christian Church. For just as Karl Barth insists that he is not a Barthian, so Jesus is certainly not a Christian –

the invisible line around the Church that divides Christian from non-Christian effectively keeps Him out.

There is a Church on the other side of the barricades but we do not lead it and have little chance of influencing it. It is led by hungry men for hungry men who name the name of Jesus only as a blasphemy at the cruel injustice of their fate. Like the New Testament Church it has little by way of form or order, and like the New Testament Church it is an untidy huddle of men seeking shelter from Principalities and Powers. Jesus, I am sure, will accept their blasphemy as adoration for it is the cry of men who live always at the end of their tether and who know not where to turn – the precise material of the Kingdom of God in fact.

When the Church on our side of the barricades finally expires, the post-mortem finding will be that we died of gluttony, choked by our surfeit of power and wealth and knowledge, as Henry the Eighth is supposed to have died of a surfeit of lampreys.

'What can we be expected to do about a complex problem like hunger?' we retort in justifiable exasperation. World poverty is an issue way beyond the resources of any Church or all the Churches. It is a world problem that only the harnessing of a world-will can solve. Only too true. But we are judged not because we have not solved the problem but because we haven't taken the pathetically inadequate first step, throwing our widow's mite into the kitty.

There is in *Letters and Papers from Prison*, the draft outline of a book Bonhoeffer did not live to write. After a section dealing with a stock-taking of Christianity, he draws the conclusion that the Church is only the Church when it exists for others. (Very proper too!

Haven't we said just that, often?) He then claims that the first step is for the Church to dispose of all its property for the benefit of those in dire need. This proposal is described by one of the scholars making a comfortable living out of analysing Bonhoeffer's thought as 'eccentric and naive'. And as someone with pretensions to a training in economics, I must agree. It *is* eccentric and naive. It is a stop-gap measure that would only touch the fringe of the problem.

Yet as a Christian I am forced to bend my attention not to world problems but specific people. Whether you regard Bonhoeffer's proposal as naive depends very much on the child it is whose belly is swelling and whose hair is dropping out before your eyes. If it were yours, would you throw the proceeds from some sale back in the Church's face and with simple faith declare 'No! Restore your York Minster! After all, my son has only a life expectancy in the early twenties even if he lives, whereas that great edifice will stand to the glory of God for the ages!' Like hell we would! We would snatch the money with greedy hands. And rightly so. For all the architectural glories of Christendom are not worth the life of a single child.

The Church is dying because it is concerned more with the salvation of the world than with half a dozen actual people. It is dying because its theological perspective is so immense and its sense of mission so destiny-filled that it must preserve itself for the ages instead of spending itself in the present. What's all that about losing our lives in order to save them? The disposal of the Church's resources is a careful operation concerned with a nice assessment of how much we can spend on others without actually damaging our basic framework. For most of us ministers, losing our lives for

Christ's sake is a willingness to live under conditions of faded gentility rather than enjoying the secular salary-spiral of the West. And sacrifice for many laymen means the offer of a reasonable slice of an adequate if not substantial income, short of the point at which our own family might suffer.

Compared with those hungry millions, the Church is as rich as Croesus and as money-conscious as Midas. We are a rich Church in a hungry world. That is why our message rings hollow and our influence declines. You can have a socialist millionaire or a mill-owning Labour supporter or a Duke who is a boot-black. But you cannot have a rich Church in a hungry world. And wealth in this context is a single penny more than it costs us to keep body and soul alive.

I do not for a second imagine that ridding ourselves of our assets will have men in their thousands turning to us in gratitude and praise to God. It is more likely they will gobble up greedily what we give them and ask for more. We shall die on this side of the barricade whatever we do. The only difference is that we would die with clean hands and quiet consciences, in a burst of profligacy which might be one of the few things about us that Jesus would recognize as His own. Otherwise we shall die in comfort by inches like the retired inmates of some seaside residential hotel.

# *Five*

NOTHING angers the faithful layman so much as all this Death-of-the-Church talk, and understandably so. 'There's enough gloom about,' he claims. 'Can't we hear a note of certainty and hope?' He has the right to ask. After all, he has invested much of his time, energy and money in Bethesda Chapel or St Mark's at the bottom of the street. It isn't very encouraging to have a parson reading the Burial Service over a patient whose loving children are struggling to keep him breathing.

Yet it is true. Every signpost at the crossroads where the Church now stands points to the cemetery. As our Eastern friends would say: *it is written.* The Church bears the mark of Death on her forehead. If she does not follow her Lord in embracing a death willingly accomplished, then she will suffer the fate of those He said were destined to lose their lives in the process of trying to save them. There are no other alternatives.

What, after all, is the Church *for*? She does not exist to put across a message to those who have not heard it or stand for an idea that the world might otherwise ignore. She exists to report an Event by *re-enacting it.*

She bears witness to God's self-revelation in the life, death and resurrection of Jesus by going through the same process herself. But her claim to be carrying on the mission of Jesus is ignored because she does not suffer the same fate. She does not die and, therefore, her preaching of the Resurrection and the triumph of God's purposes against all odds is mere speech blown away by the wind. The only proof of Resurrection is a genuine crucifixion, a certified death and an empty tomb.

The world may be bored by our preaching and dismiss our Gospel as meaningless but at least it knows that Jesus *died* because of what He said and did. So, by simple logic, any institution which talks of being the Body of Christ and of extending His ministry ought also to die. If it does not, then its proud claims can rightly be dismissed as presumption and vanity. Subject to death by organic decay when its time is over, it must be classed with any other human institution. And is this not precisely what is happening? The decline of the Church becomes apparent as soon as she loses her virtual monopoly of wealth, knowledge and power, and must live by her merits in a world which sneers at mystiques and judges solely by performance.

'Forbid it, Lord, that I should boast, save in the death of Christ, my Lord . . .' runs a line of the well-loved hymn. It is doubtful whether we ought even to boast about *that* unless we can match the feat ourselves. All the confident claims in our liturgy about the Church's ability to triumph over adversity and prevail against the gates of Hell are much like the bragging of a man in a pub that he intends to go over Niagara Falls in a barrel. It is assumed that it is the wine talking until he is seen boarding ship at Southampton lugging a barrel. Then his fellow revellers are not quite so sure. Equally, a style of life that runs counter to the laws governing the survival of any other human institution – prudence, investment, hoarding, reserve – would spell out the Church's confidence that when she is utterly spent, God will call her forth again, like Lazarus, from the tomb. Until that time, we have no complaint if the world assumes that it is just the communion wine talking when we utter our more extravagant claims.

But either way it is death, just as either way it was death for Jesus. Had He brushed aside the cup His Father placed before Him in Gethsemane, He would still have died. Full of years and honour, possibly; but sooner or later the clay finger of death would have turned Him to dust. Like all the great of this world He would now be enbalmed in human memory and the pages of history books. He lives because He died and He rises glorious because He died willingly.

The Church bears the marks of that other, creeping death, because she has brushed aside the cup that Jesus drank. This is why there is about her the pervasive smell of senility, the dogged pernicketiness of the aged, the compulsive chatter about past great days, the sad bewilderment at the evil of the present time. She sits rocking in her favourite chair, nodding off from time to time, croaking good advice to the laughing young which they listen to with the deference due to the aged – then ignore.

Little men with shrunken bellies call the Church's bluff. They challenge her to put her immortality to the test for they are the visible tip of a vast iceberg of human need. All round is a great sea of outstretched hands and open mouths that would devour all the

Church's wealth and time and love. To answer that challenge seriously must spell the death of the institutional Church. She would die for lack of funds to pay her way, shortage of the manpower necessary to maintain even a skeleton administration and wilful neglect of her property, most of which she would forfeit anyway when the mortgage became due.

But we brush the cup aside. We don't die. It is the little man who dies instead. And so we lose the chance to discover the answer to the only ecclesiastical question that matters: if the Church dies, shall she rise again, and in what form? All property, said Proudhon, is theft. The simple observable fact of the little man's poverty and the Church's wealth is evidence of robbery, the despoiling of God's Creation: in the case of the Church, a crime as despicable as that of a son who rifles his mother's purse. That the Church connives by silence when strong men loot the universe is utterly wrong; that she carries away her own share of the spoils is unforgivable.

When men fear death and seek to stave it off, they resort to magic. This is what we have done by our ritualizing of Christ's death, our invocation of a magical rite at altar and communion table. The bits of bread and drops of wine, whatever words we recite over them, are substitutes for *our* flesh and blood, not Christ's. We do not enter into the sacrifice of Jesus by going through the motions of a tea party but by offering to Him our own broken bodies and poured out lives. These are the only true sacramental elements.

We ritualize the death of Jesus because we dare not share it. We take part in the ceremonial like the hale and hearty young men of an African tribe who cover themselves with ashes and lie prone alongside the body of their dead chief. It is not for real. They know it and so do all the onlookers. Tomorrow they will be back at their hunting, fishing, laughing and loving.

The best sacramental theology seeks to see the Church as a company sealed with Christ in His death. At the hour of Eucharist, says the Bishop of Woolwich, the Church is a great charnel house with the altar as a butcher's slab. But we are playing word games again. Once the ritual of death is over, the trustees will be worrying over the leaking roof and rusty boiler, the parson will agonize over the state of the Church's finances and the congregation will be complaining about the draught, the peeling paint and the length of the sermon. Such rites of preservation *are* for real. We act upon them. That ritual of death we call Holy Communion has relevance for most Christians only in the sphere of private devotion. It does not edge the Church one inch nearer her death. Indeed, sacramental revival is seen by some churchmen as the Church's best hope of survival.

Because we are frantically struggling to repair cracks in the Church's chrysalis, we are blind to the butterfly inside waiting to break out and fly. Though the institutional Church is decaying, she is still massive enough to obscure the view of a whole world around us slowly materializing as the Body of Christ, with honest politicians for saints, seekers after truth as priests, writers and artists and film-makers as preachers and with flower children, civil rights marchers and crackpot advocates of total disarmament and world government as martyrs. And the baptized are those who spend themselves in meeting human need, repairing the ravages wrought to God's creation by the brutalizing of man.

A New Humanity is taking shape before our eyes.

The old frontier between those who acknowledge Christ and those who reject Him has gone. The new one marks off those who stand for man from those who reject him, those who affirm life from those who deny it. That frontier runs as much through the institutional Church as any other part of our society. For all the misery, frustration and anguish of our world, there are forces at work seeking to re-humanize man, restore to him the dignity in which God first clothed him and revitalize jaded cultures and decadent societies. Christ's New Man does not talk *about* God but *to* his neighbour. He seeks God not by spiritual exploration but by asking questions about the meaning of life. He has not renounced Christian asceticism but transformed it; he mortifies his body not for the good of his soul but to meet another's need.

To stand for and within this New Humanity is not, for the Christian at least, a commitment to any ideal of human progress. The goal is not Utopia or Shangri-La but a Kingdom inherited through sacrifices and the creative power of suffering. Everything is for, through and in Jesus. When men discover their manhood again by solving the problems of every day existence, in such a way that no one is excluded from the feast of life, they will find that the fullness of all they have struggled to achieve is demonstrated to perfection in Jesus. Though they never breathe His name, they will be like Him. For they will have been baptized with the baptism wherewith He was baptized.

Not until the Church dies will we be able to look beyond the cut-down Christ imprisoned within it and share the vision of Teilhard de Chardin of a Jesus graven across the universe, the crown of a great growing, converging movement of all things from the tiniest

73

stirrings in the dark before history to their culmination in the Kingdom, the Power and the Glory. In this majestic procession nothing and no one standing for life is rejected but swept up, transformed and built into the structure of the Kingdom. Struggling to keep our heads above water in this cosmic tide-race we shall find ourselves accompanied by some strange fellow-voyagers. The most we can do is greet them and clasp hands for an instant when we are thrown together in the swell. The truly tragic ones are those we shall meet fighting grimly to make their way against the current, towards death and the past, crying their rejection of life all the while. Unhappily, many of them will, with heroically misplaced energy, be trying to manhandle the institutional Church up-stream with them.

The little man not only shows how the Church can achieve her death but also is our link with the New Humanity. We reach out for Jesus within the New Humanity not by accepting a total theological system but at the precise instant that we do what Jesus commands and answer the need of the little people of the earth. And we remain of His company only for as long as we go on doing it. There is a whole theology in the costly deed. It takes all the grace of God to make me *see* my neighbour and the whole Gospel, Creation, Redemption and Judgement are proclaimed when I act upon what I see. The cost is heavy but the rewards are great. The little man is the key to freedom and true humility, and to that intensifying of consciousness that once could only be achieved by spiritual introspection. As my neighbour, he is the answer to every question that really matters, and yet in turn poses enough questions of his own to keep me loving the Lord with all my mind for life.

The old rabbis used to say that the Kingdom of God would come if only the whole of Israel would really keep a single Sabbath simultaneously. Possibly mankind will only cross the watershed from death to life when the whole Church abandons prudence and unleashes the totality of her resources in a great burst of compassion. She ought to do it because she never ceases to proclaim the fact that this is what she is for, and she can best do it because she is the only institution in the modern world which is totally expendable, that can, without irresponsibility, go out in a great explosion of flaming love. She has no dependents, no contractual obligations, no future engagements that must be honoured. There would be no crater left where she had been, just as there was no residue of human clay left behind when Lazarus came forth from the tomb.

It is death either way. The willing acceptance of an accomplished death would at least ensure that there was a Body left for God, if He so willed, to transfigure. The other way, our present course, means slow erosion, gradual shrinkage, until the Church's bones are laid to rest in the cemetery of lost causes, ancient glories and faded dreams.

# *Six*

To talk of sharing the anonymous ministry of Jesus in the world must raise the whole question of prayer. I can follow Jesus in the sense of trying to do as He did as a programme of action but if He has any kind of present reality I must be able to make contact, to commune with Him. For me, prayer, as talking to an invisible Being from out of the world, is not an open option, though I do not presume to question the reality of the traditional spiritual life for others. The whole area of experience we call prayer must have some place in the life of the radical Christian; otherwise obedience to Christ will degenerate into mere ethics tinged with concern or humanitarianism with a religious label.

The essential clue is found in the fact that my particular meeting with the hungry little man brought me up against a mystery. It is not just that his plight raises economic, political and moral issues I must try to puzzle through. His essence as a person stays tantalizingly just outside the reach of my understanding. He enshrines some truth that I cannot put into words. I find myself, like Coventry Patmore, as one who knows a tune and cannot sing. He has, and is, so little in a human sense that he cannot teach me anything or give me anything – yet when I stand in his presence I become something. His need is so glaring and my ability to meet it so obvious that our true inter-dependence is established in a flash. He can no more do without me than I can do without him. To face him squarely without flinching takes both moral courage to grieve at his condition and religious courage to rejoice that in his gaunt frame there still burns life – that bare, raw life found only on the frontier, a hair's breadth across, which divides the only just living from the terribly dead.

All our meetings are not of this sort. Our nervous systems would explode if they were. We pass hundreds in the street, share a road with dozens and even live with a few without seeing them as mysteries. They are what they are, described and dismissed in our working shorthand as a *crowd*, our *neighbours*, the *family*. But now and again, we are taken hold of and forced to look someone in the eye. They stand out from the rest of the crowd by virtue of something that lights them from within. We feel the impact of their personalities upon us as though struck by a blow. He is not just a man but Man, the one who stands for and explains the rest. Man stripped down to the bare essentials, a ragged shirt, a pair of shorts and an empty biro pen. He is not Man hidden behind and projected through a multitude of possessions, but naked Man, as he is in himself.

Such moments of truth are unrepeatable. We only walk the Emmaus road with this stranger once. Rabbi Nahman said 'God does not do the same thing twice.' The little man is unique. No one in the world has ever embodied his particular truth. Otherwise there would have been no need for him to exist. Why did he exist? He cannot have been created to spend his days scavenging on the garbage heaps of life and die unnoticed. If so, what a monstrous universe! If not, what a moral revolution is required, revolution in the name of personality to overthrow the idols of race, nationalisms, economics, techniques and production – to smash down the supremacy of things.

It is at such moments that we echo Berdyaev's claim that every single human soul has more meaning and value than the whole of history with its empires, its wars and revolutions, its blossoming and fading Civilizations. We will not make sense of this world or even get within reaching distance of blotting out its scourges until we can concentrate with a kind of desperate urgency upon single human beings; until there is brought home to us, at a level deeper than our minds, the miracle of one man's life. the mystery of his being and the outrage of an eternal spirit beaten down to the animal level of life by other eternal spirits.

There was no sentimentality about my encounter with the hungry little man. I have seen too many like him, and sensitivity is soon blunted when horror is a daily experience. I was drawn to him in spite of my all too human disgust at his filth and smell and the parody of a true man he presented. It was not pity, for that would have been called out by *his* need, whereas in some strange way the effect he had was to underline *my* need. He made me conscious of being deprived of something precious, of being cut off from the place where the action of life is. He exposed the utter idiocy of relative terms like *wealth* and *poverty*. In his lack of virtually anything we would claim necessary for life, he proved that a man only has the wealth he is, the beauty that he lives and the truth revealed in the bare fact that he is there.

It would be hypocrisy to suggest that I had any desire to share his life. I couldn't. I am not made of the stuff of those who can sell all and throw themselves on the mercy of others for a crust of bread, a place to lay one's head and a shirt to one's back. This, I suspect, is not so much fear of hardship as pride, the rejection of utter dependence upon others – the thing more than anything else which stops us from following Jesus.

A special kind of grace operates on the boundary – the power to celebrate life common to those who have nothing else. This surprising quality possessed by many who do not know where their next meal is coming from is not irresponsibility but gratitude. Whatever they do not possess, they do possess the gift of life itself and that is compensation for much that is denied them. Certainly there is ugliness, degradation and viciousness at this level of existence but also a kind of wonder which Western man has lost because he meets life only indirectly through a multiplicity of things. His appetites become jaded and his values insecure. In contrast, nothing protected my little man from the raw lick of life. He shivered in the cold and glowed in the warmth of the sun and blessed or cursed a shower of rain according to whether his greatest need at the moment was for a drink of water or a roof over his head.

It was his acceptance of the sheer *givenness* of life that called out in me a quality I can only describe as reverence. I was drawn to him as those equally starved of life were drawn to Jesus of Nazareth. Jesus had crossed my path, not Jesus *in* the little man or Jesus *working through* him, but for the purposes of devotion he

79

*was* Jesus in His totality. There was no Other, invisible Being standing outside us. I was in the place and attitude of prayer because I was face to face with divinity, seeing the essence of Life.

A truly secular devotion requires that I should believe that the entire Being of God encountered me in the little man. *At that moment*, he was all there was of the Christian God.

Such flashes of insight can easily be trivialized when put into words and seem merely a daring way of talking. For most of us, the truth of the Word made Flesh is treated as a metaphor of God's action, a vivid way of picturing God at work in the life of the world and of our fellow men. But it is easy to test whether we talk literally or metaphorically about the Word made flesh in a hungry little man, by our mode of address to him. An Indian greeted a soldier who, at the time of the Indian Mutiny, was about to put a bayonet in his body, with the words 'And thou too art divine'. That's it. Dare I, when I have such a soul-shaking encounter, cry 'My Lord and my God!' or am I afraid of uttering the ultimate blasphemy? Is it seriously believable that at that moment there is no Jesus for me anywhere else in the universe, that Heaven is empty, or more correctly, is located at the precise spot on which the little man is standing?

There are many reasons why one would hesitate to make an absolute identification of Jesus with this mysterious little man. For one thing, in his misery he is prone to say and do what by any Biblical standard is plain evil. He is often demonic in his despair and can show a frightening malevolence. Indeed, he is capable of doing what Jesus refused to do – curse God and die. Would not the distinction between good and evil lose all significance if Jesus were materialized in him not as spirit but as personality?

Reconciling the existence of evil with the nature of God has always been one of the less successful efforts of orthodox theology. Most explanations strain our credulity to the limit and sound very unconvincing indeed when offered to those who do not believe. Secular devotion, far from playing down the reality of evil, must accept a deepening of its mystery as taken up into the very nature of God. Possibly that darkness the light shines out of, about which Paul talks, is even thicker than traditional spirituality believes. If God is present for all time in us we must be prepared for the shock of His dealing with evil not somewhere beyond our ken but right in front of our faces. Can we conceive of a Jesus whose identification with a man is so complete that He echoes his blasphemies?

If the hungry man *is* Jesus for me at a given moment, I must either face up to a far from sinless Jesus or redefine the meaning of sin and grace. This is no new problem of course. It has always lurked just beneath the surface whenever the orthodox Christian has talked of Jesus *in* him. If this means more than doing and saying things that are recognizably Christian; if it suggests some interior occupation by the personality of Jesus, his evil actions take some explanation. It is not enough to say that the good a man does is owed to the Jesus within whilst the evil is the outworking of his own lower nature.

To be a person is to have a single centre of consciousness from which all actions good and bad stem. If Jesus takes possession of this centre of consciousness then the person *becomes* Jesus. If, on the other hand, he adds an extra Jesus-centre of consciousness, he ceases to be a human person. When Paul cries 'I live, yet not

I, Christ lives in me!' that is powerful devotion but a psychological impossibility on any modern understanding of personality. For Paul could only have had one centre of consciousness. Either he thought of himself as Paul or he thought of himself as Jesus. And either Paul or Jesus was responsible for his various actions, but not a mixture of both. Therefore, if Jesus truly dwells in us, He must take responsibility for actions and thoughts which are evil, or else such phrases as 'Christ in you, the hope of glory' must be seen as picture language and not literal truth.

So either way – Jesus *in* a man or a man *as* Jesus at a given moment – evil remains an intractable problem. I prefer to believe that when the one I acknowledge at any time as Jesus for me does or says what is evil I must accept it as from Jesus as a mystery and see its purpose as the enrichment of my life through the struggle to overcome it by love.

Such an identification of Jesus with my little man also invites the charge of pantheism – God as everything and utterly mixed up in and undistinguished from His creation. I have no defence, except to point out that this pantheism is radically different from the impersonal Life-force which is its traditional guise. Jesus, whom I recognize because of a historical life, does not confront me as an impersonal force but in the shockingly personal form of a Zambian beggar. Indeed, is not this the very opposite of pantheism? Not God as everything, but God as one thing at one time, or rather one personality – the Word made flesh, in fact.

It is a combination of pride and unbelief that has us imagining that the reality of Jesus depends upon some correct way of thinking about Him, some orthodoxy that we ourselves have laid down. When God refused to disclose His name to the Jews, He was warning men against manufacturing *any* idols, whether material objects or intellectual systems. Jesus has given us the freedom to be both rigorously agnostic and insatiably curious. And the community which bears His name exists to promote free enquiry, not to defend some orthodoxy. No doors are closed to us. No thoughts are forbidden. We can explore any system or philosophy or idea fearlessly and judge the truth or lie in it according to the single standard that it helps us to get at the meaning of Jesus in the concrete event. Jesus is well able to take care of Himself. He can safeguard His identity and burst through all mistaken conceptions of Himself when the need arises. After all, we are in His hands, not He in ours.

The test of truly secular prayer is the willingness to abandon any address to an invisible Third Party. This is where I find books of contemporary prayers by such men as Michel Quoist and Malcolm Boyd vaguely unsatisfying if very moving. The language is unflinchingly realistic and the imagery is stark and shocking. Ye there is still the invocation of an invisible Jesus who stands by the shoulder of the one who prays and has His attention drawn to the joys and horrors of the world: 'Lord, I am ashamed of this magazine. You must be profoundly hurt in your infinite purity . . . and yet, Lord, man's body is beautiful . . .' runs one of Michel Quoist's prayers about pornography. Jesus seems to be a Divine Spectator. It is traditional prayer in a secular mould. If that is the intention, well and good, many will find new life blowing through a usually arid corner of their experience. My problem is different. How can I pray, not to an invisible Third Party *about* the little man but *to* him as Jesus?

I can only take the risk and address him directly. Prayer is my total response to him in action, feeling and speech, my revulsion as much as my compassion, my anger at his importunity as much as my openness to his need. It is Jesus who thanks or curses me and throws the bread back in my face. It is Jesus who damns my health and wealth or leers and pleads with me. What He says and does when I address Him may be hard or incomprehensible or even irrelevant, but that is the answer to my prayer and I must make of it what I can.

This way is the way of pain and discomfort, the destruction of all neat pigeon-holes, all tidy explanations and lucid blueprints. It is the way of confusion and untidiness, a great sprawling mixture of Jesus, the world and me, inextricable and without clearly distinguished identity – in fact, that glorious inter-penetration described by Angelus Silesius as 'God, the fire in me, I the glow in Him. . . .'

This is the time of the death of all orthodoxies and the destruction of all temples. The forces of a secular age have not destroyed Jesus; rather they have, by smashing the moulds of a 4th century world-view, given Christians the creative freedom to find Jesus anywhere and in any form. The Temple, the place of prayer, is that particular spot where vision, action and devotion are united. Heresy is inevitable, but then I doubt that anyone can make a personal discovery of Jesus without falling into at least one serious heresy, for the world, reality, life – where Jesus is – does not fit neatly into any dogma's description of it. Indeed, it is doubtful whether it is possible to talk any longer meaningfully about heresy. You can only declare a man a heretic if you are certain you have the truth yourself. And since God, however He is conceived, can only be the Object of faith, it is rating your guesses pretty high to burn someone at the stake or excommunicate him because he chooses the Jesus he has found in preference to the One you tell him he must believe in.

What, then, does sanctity mean in this scheme of things? What are the marks of the saint, the end product of a devotional life? It must be a robustly political style of life. I glorify Jesus by transfiguring the life of the little man in whom He materializes. This cannot be done by acts of compassion alone, for he is the victim of a whole complexity of economic and political forces that brutalize him. If he is to be transfigured, society must be restructured. If the traditional saint affirms a mysticism of love, the secular saint affirms a mysticism of freedom and justice.

All the masters of Devotion have stressed the importance of personal discipline as necessary to maintain an attitude of spiritual introspection in the face of worldly distractions. The secular saint also has need of discipline to do the precise opposite, to keep his face squarely towards the world against the lure of spiritual introspection; to prevent him from hiving off into closed systems of piety, the search for a spiritualized God, the hunt for Jesus in religion instead of hungry little men.

The secular saint is necessarily a man of affairs, dealing much of his time with the bread and butter issues of life but he must also exercise two spiritual qualities that together form the basis of what might be called political mysticism. They are awe and faith. Awe is the appropriate attitude for those who deal in power. They become dangerous if ever they get over their wonder that others trust them with power or their amazement that in spite of what they know of themselves they still use it justly on the whole. And without faith, politics is impossible. No political judgement is cut and dried. It is proved good or bad only by its consequences. Hence, political activity requires faith that men will prove consistent and predictable and willing to live with the results of other men's planning without trying to change things by violence to suit their own advantage.

Whoever would tinker with the world, as a politician must, needs faith that things hold together, that change at any point will not cause everything else to fly apart. This must be a matter of faith because there is something in human life and human history which cannot be reduced to scientific rule. The theologian calls this the realm of the sacred, that which is and will always remain outside our control and understanding. In spite of our vast knowledge, this unexplorable area does not get less. The man of action must have faith that this realm is benevolent, that dark forces do not originate from it which will work against him and bring his efforts to nothing.

Such uses of traditional spiritual qualities may be novel but they are necessary if politics is to work for man and not against him.

The unitary vision of the traditional mystic also has its counterpart in secular devotion. Again, the idiom is political. The only unity the modern world possesses is functional, the bringing together of a variety of independent skills and activities to solve specific problems. Politics is both the way things happen and the way a society understands itself in a time when there is no supernational point of focus to which everything and every activity can be related. Individuals and groups come together from many directions and points of interest to transform human life. Unity is not in *seeing* things whole, but in the attempt to *make* them whole.

Religious vocation in the sense of life-commitment to a cause is a rarity in this world. Men will take up tasks that seem worthwhile, do them as best they can and remain uncommitted beyond the end of the job. This may be said from the Church's point of view when it leads to a drying up of the supply of ministers or missionaries or candidates for religious orders. But it is the way of a world in revolution and the secular saint says Yes to it in response to the God who is overthrowing all systems including the theological ones that seek to explain Him. In the midst of this confusion, vision is often restricted and fragmentary; for much of the time we have got to recognize that we no longer know God and be content that He knows us.

# Seven

THOUGH the little man with the shrunken belly has scorched my conscience, he has at least freed me from my faithless worrying about the survival of the Church. Only when I sit down and think it out coldly do I realize how much of my time and energy has gone into puzzling out how the Church can *win*. Much of my preaching, praying and reading has centred round this theme. Indeed, are not most of our efforts to make the Gospel plain to modern man, our juggling around with images of God, really strategies for the survival of the Church?

Now I know that the survival which counts is not that of the Church but of the little man with the shrunken belly. We in the West have not been totally oblivious of his need. We have carefully set out our stall and offered him a choice between Rome or Canterbury, Washington or Moscow, capitalism or communism. He chose something else – life – and had to accept death. It was his right. Jesus willed him abundant life. The Church, as our Lord's executor, tried to fob him off with promises he did not live to redeem, assurances that came to nothing, fervent concern that added not one moment to his life.

In his death, the whole purpose of Creation was frustrated and the Church bears unlimited responsibility, for has she not for centuries trumpeted her guardianship of the little people of the earth? Have we not echoed the claim of Jesus: 'The Spirit of the Lord is upon me, because he has anointed me to preach good tidings to the poor: He has sent me to heal the broken hearted, to proclaim release to the captives, and recovering of sight to the blind, to set at liberty them that are bruised, to proclaim the acceptable year of the Lord.'

What is our traditional insistence worth that we put the widow, the orphan, the hungry and homeless at the centre of our concern? Long ago, we staked our claim to the constituency of the world's unwanted. If our interest has shifted, or we can no longer make good our promise to keep hungry men alive, we should get out of the way and let someone else try. In gambling slang, if we cannot put up, then we should shut up.

Honourable failure is one thing. If we have given all and it is not enough, then we have no cause to reproach ourselves. But our failure has not been honourable. The Church has succumbed to that disease of senility, hoarding. We have stored away our substance, building ever bigger barns, paying out our resources with judicious care within the framework of certified balance-sheets, weighing what we can afford to give today against the needs of tomorrow.

The Church has no tomorrows. She is called to live at Golgotha where men do not die a little or suffer minimally but breathe their last, having used up all their life. Tomorrow is the time God speaks a new word which may or may not be addressed to the Church, to call her out of the tomb. We are without honour because we have not used up all that God has given us to heal the wounds of our time, to keep alive at least some hungry little men.

As a Methodist I am without excuse for ignoring this truth. For I am a son of a prophetic movement which became an institution by mistake. Much has been written about John Wesley as an inspired opportunist who worked out the Methodist 'system' piece-meal, in the saddle as it were, in solving the problems that a particular time threw at him as he sought to identify himself with what God was doing. Thus, John Vincent again: 'Wesley "submitted to become more vile" and went to preach in the open air, because people were not allowed to hear him inside a Church. Thus did lay preachers receive permission to preach because Wesley's mother assured him that to oppose it would be to oppose God. Thus were all and sundry admitted to the Communion as it proved to be "itself a converting ordinance". Thus did the Circuit system arise purely as a convenient unity within which preachers might have a "round". Thus did Wesley ordain others because the crying need of his people for the sacraments could not be met in any other way. Thus did the Class Meeting begin, in part at least, as a means of financing the work through the weekly "Class money". . . .'

On this reading of Methodist history, it is as profitless for staunch Methodists now to be fighting a last ditch battle to preserve these distinctive Wesleyan emphases as it would be to recreate the structures of eighteenth century politics or the tribal mechanisms of the Kingdom of Monomatopa, which flourished in Africa around the time Wesley was preaching. Prophecy cannot be inherited. It is currency which can only be spent, not invested. It cannot be passed from generation to generation preserved in Church Order or a theological system or volumes of sermons. It is a God-given faculty for seeing to the heart of a particular age. We can no more preserve it or re-incarnate it in a situation remote from its time than we could recapture the jubilation of the victory at Trafalgar or the horror of the Great Plague. When we try, we are smothered in debris – dogma as the corpse of dead prophecy, the husk of an institutional Church, the left-overs of someone else's party, the faded notes of someone else's sermon.

Prophetic movements cannot be rejuvenated by jazzing up doctrine or streamlining policy. If any time is left to them, they are only galvanized into life by the shock of falling across the terminals of Jesus' love and human need, taking the full impact of the intensity of the one and the enormity of the other. They materialize in the form best suited to meeting the particular claim upon their compassion and not in the shapes of historically received dogma. They are as free as their Lord from the dead-weight of the past to be what men need where they stand.

Only by concentrating with a kind of savage desperation upon individual people can the Church combat the deadening effects of institutionalism. And this can only mean sharing their life-substance. We are in error when we see our relationship to men and women primarily in terms of a message we have to deliver to them. Not since Old Testament times has God communicated to men by means of messages. In the New Testament, the message God communicates is Himself by the act of entering history and immersing Himself in the life-substance of humanity. That is still the way it is done. Christianity is first, last and all the time, personal encounter, and anything which takes the place of or prevents direct confrontation nullifies the whole thing.

The peril of all ecclesiastical structures is that they come between man and man and protect those within from the pain and cost of personal encounter with those outside. When men find themselves promoting Christianity from inside buildings, behind desks, on the other side of lecterns, through sets of account books, by means of textbooks, the scale of the Christian enterprise greatly expands, the personal factor is played down and the feeding of hungry little men tends to become a strategy instead of an act of costly compassion. The price of humane service is swallowed up in the overheads instead of paid for in personal discipleship.

It would be silly to suggest that any continuing form of human co-operation can get along without a structure of some kind. If a good one is not purposely created, a ramshackle one will grow haphazardly. But when that organization is a Church, she ought never to forget the judgement implied in the need for a structure. It is a material sign of our lack of faith, our reliance upon the principles of administration and good business instead of looking solely to Jesus to keep our heads above water.

Leo Tolstoy, who was a fierce and implacable enemy of all that worked against human encounter and creativity, once described in the context of Government how the institution enables men to countenance actions they would shrink from carrying through if they were face to face with people: 'Some men write the laws, others apply them; a third set drill men and habituate them to discipline, that is to say to senseless and implicit obedience; a fourth set – the people who are disciplined commit all kinds of deeds without knowing why or wherefore. But a man need only for a moment free himself mentally from this net of worldly organization in which he is involved to understand the unnaturalness of what he has done. . . .'

Tolstoy was writing, of course, about how evil can be done within the framework of good order because the distance between the commissioning of the deed and its execution robs it of all horror. But his illustration can be used to show how prone compassion at a distance is to change its character, and love get mislaid somewhere in a maze of corridors, a sheaf of minutes or a filing cabinet.

Savage concentration upon hungry little men is the only way to stop them being fed into modern compassion-machines to emerge as 'issues'. A U.S. correspondent in the *Saturday Evening Post* quotes an American officer in Viet Nam as saying: 'We've killed a lot of friendly people, and I'm real sorry. But like Sherman said, "War is hell".' That is how it is done; that is how you can sleep at night and live with your conscience. War is an industry, an institution, a massive enterprise able to absorb endless suffering and transform it into necessity. War is what happens to abstractions. Murder is the correct word for what happened to those 'friendly people'. The institution destroys the character of human qualities like love and hate by breaking them down into so many components that they are no longer recognizable. So we can do evil with a quiet conscience and dole out love without personal cost.

Institutionalizing our compassion is one way of neglecting hungry little men. Mechanizing our message is the other. We are in the communications business in a big way. The exponents of modern evangelism urge upon us the use of every technique of communication to get the Gospel across – radio, television, literature, advertising. It is as well for us to recognize what we are really doing. All techniques of communications, as Marshall McLuhan has analysed them, are extensions of the human senses – print and camera of the eye, telephone and radio of the ear, electronic devices of the central nervous system. By their aid we can put across a message without personal involvement. We need not be there. We can tell the whole globe about the sacrificial love of God without it costing us anything more than the breath we expend. It is love at a distance again. We are at the other end of the microphone, the television camera or the printing presses. No one can tap us on the shoulder and say 'Prove it!' We are beyond reach. Radio will amplify our voices until they reverberate to the ends of the earth and television will multiply our image by millions, but we might well be on another planet. We have torn apart the unity of word and action personified by Jesus. We have gone back to the Old Testament where Jehovah thundered words from Mount Horeb instead of to the New Testament where Jesus shared the life-substance of the sick, the leprous, the demon-ridden. They could reach out and touch Him and the healing was in the contact.

Is it an utterly outrageous thought that needy humanity began to slip from its central place in the Church's heart when the Gospel was first reduced to writing, when a man need no longer look another in the eye and say 'The Man Jesus whom I follow has commanded me to love you as myself' and could instead say 'Read all about it!'? Possibly a link in the chain of the Apostolic Succession snapped at that point. Hundreds of men could read of Jesus at the same time, and thousands have the Gospel read out to them. The cells of the Christian organism rapidly multiplied but the minimum cost of personal discipleship was drastically reduced. The wide-ranging communication of the Gospel enabled whole communities to be baptized into the name of Jesus and thus set the Church on the road to becoming a powerful institution, instead of remaining a small minority of personal witnesses in whom word and act were perfectly joined.

Hungry little men do not merely test our compassion, they embody our Judgement. History does not make much sense unless our Lord returns in glory, bringing transparent clarity to the affairs of men and nations, tearing aside all veils, restoring all that has been destroyed, casting down the proud and lifting up the oppressed. It is dangerous to assume that we shall be given ample warning of this Event by some kind of heavenly firework display as described in Charles Wesley's hymn 'Lo! He comes with clouds descending!' There is another strand of Biblical truth which speaks of our Lord slipping back into history, furtively, like a burglar in the dark, and confronting us. But how?

From what we know of the historical Jesus we can be fairly sure that the One who is always sneaking back into history will stand before us in the form of the casualties of this world, the lonely, hungry, broken, imprisoned, outcast – those right under our nose we tend not to see or whose plight is too painful for us to contemplate. I would be wise to act always as though any encounter with the humanly deprived embodied my destiny – 'When saw we Thee hungry or thirsty or naked. . . ?' When else but driving through an African village, pushing our way through the crowded streets of an Asian city, hurrying past the seedier parts of our own town or glancing casually at an Oxfam advertisement? The air is alive with Judgement. Wherever we turn we see the pitiful form of the One who shall Come.

If it is possible to make sense of a world that brutalizes millions then Jesus is the sense of it. And Jesus is all the Church has got left. Much of our dogma is not believed because it is just not believable. Fourth century formulations of doctrine were honourable attempts to universalize the Christ of the Jews using the *ecumenical* currency of Greek thought. That philosophical coinage is no more legal tender in the modern world than stones with holes in them or monster cowrie-shells. The Creeds and the classical statements of doctrine describe the way men of a time saw Jesus, and because they were holier and wiser than ourselves we do well to study them carefully. The issues they raised are for all time; their answers primarily for their own time.

To test who is of Christ by demanding assent to the letter of dogma is asking modern man to renounce his world and his right to keep his face toward the future. It locates the Kingdom of God in the past, which is bad, and identifies the Church with the Kingdom, which is worse.

We are free, and indeed have a duty to make our own discovery of Jesus. This is the only possible starting point for theological renewal – not a streamlining of what Christians ought to believe nor what is believable in the sense of being brought into line with modern thought, but what they actually do believe – what, in short, is their experience of Christ in the concrete event.

Stripping down Christianity to what is sneeringly called a Jesus-cult need not be the first step to the nearest Unitarian church. I have found that following the way of Jesus – a combination of Christ-devotion and Christian Action – leads to a majestic conception of God. I can only discover the true significance of Jesus as Early Christians did, by being with Him as He bursts out of every inadequate way of looking at Him. The progression – Man, Master, Saviour, Lord – represents stages in a journey taken with Jesus. Relentlessly He drives me on, eluding all my efforts to pin down His essence, smashing His way out of every structure I build round Him.

Individual piety alone will not entitle me to share the Ministry of Jesus in our world. He was not a Ghost or an Enigma without ancestory but a Jew, crowning a prophetic tradition which united God-consciousness with political action to an extent unique in the history of religion. The prophets spoke of God as the agent of social and political change so drastic as to merit the name of revolution. To follow Jesus in our day is to stand within that tradition for a political radicalism that makes the most extreme political party seem pale pink.

Radical discontinuity between the past and the future alone offers any hope that the children of the hungry little man will not be even hungrier. Compassionate action for Jesus' sake could not be further removed from the 'each smile a hymn, each kindly deed a prayer' school of pietism. We dare not offer any man bread in Jesus' name without political commitment – a striving to end the political oppression and economic serfdom that brutalize men to the point where their right to life depends upon a crust of bread.

There is danger in all personal rediscoveries of Jesus. We may be dishonest or deluded in our portrayal of

Him and scale down His demands to tie in with what we can comfortably meet. Basing all our action to a personal understanding of Jesus lays us open to the egotism and partiality in our nature that distorts our vision. Yet the necessary corrective is not to dash back into the thickets of dogma and take the word of other ages for who Jesus is and what He requires. The answer, surely, is to pursue the search for Jesus in the company of others who are asking the same questions and risking the same temptations; who will offer us correction and counsel, strengthening us where we are timid and curbing us where we are extreme. Because the truth by its nature is healing and redemptive, the search for it will create genuine community rather than intensify individualism. Community of Christians is a working necessity not a dogmatic requirement.

It looks as though a fully developed theology evolves from the simplest attempt to follow Jesus in meeting human need. In *acting*, I may discover the relevance of theological themes I am prone to reject when they are hurled at me from a text book. But the important thing is to meet the need. To put theology first and make compassion an outworking of it is to imply that the theologian's work is to chart the Church's course. The true role of the theologian is to reflect upon the action of the People of God and not to initiate it.

Harvey Cox claims that it is not God who is dead, but modern theology. Both the Death of God school and its direct opponents are working in a vacuum – the one constructing theoretical iron-lungs to keep God breathing, the other gazing, hypnotized, into His grave. Both tend to be intensely religious, Church-centred and non-political.

The fault does not lie with modern theologians who

are as dedicated, scholarly and reflective as their fore-bears were. They end up as archaeologists uncovering historical origins or as scavengers of secular thought trying to tie in esoteric concepts with Biblical Faith because much of the ongoing life of the Church is too trivial to give them scope for reflection upon what is *being done* in Jesus' name.

Only when we cease to worry about strategies for the survival of the Church and bend all our attention to finding strategies for the survival of hungry little men can theology come alive again. To wait with bated breath, as many Christians seem to be doing, for the next utterance of a 'significant' theologian in the hope that he will come up with a formula for the renewal of Christianity is both futile and callow. Great theology must always be paid for in advance by costly discipleship.


All this seems to me, rightly or wrongly, to flow from my encounter with one hungry man. What begins as a charitable impulse ends in a political crusade, the acceptance of the challenge to follow Jesus, the Chaos-Bringer, as He turns our society inside out.

But for the rest of our fevered ecclesiastical concerns, I choose the way of the coward. In the evocative words of Sam Goldwyn – include me out!